Journey from Paris
to the Limousin

Journey from Paris to the Limousin

Letters to Madame de La Fontaine (1663)

Jean de La Fontaine

Translated and Edited
by Robert W. Berger

Madison • Teaneck
Fairleigh Dickinson University Press

© 2008 by Robert W. Berger

All rights reserved. Authorization to photocopy items for internal or personal use, or the internal or personal use of specific clients, is granted by the copyright owner, provided that a base fee of $10.00, plus eight cents per page, per copy is paid directly to the Copyright Clearance Center, 222 Rosewood Drive, Danvers, Massachusetts 01923. [978-0-8386-4141-5/08 $10.00 + 8¢ pp, pc.]

Associated University Presses
2010 Eastpark Boulevard
Cranbury, NJ 08512

The paper used in this publication meets the requirements of the American National Standard for Permanence of Paper for Printed Library Materials Z39.48-1984.

Library of Congress Cataloging-in-Publication Data

La Fontaine, Jean de, 1621–1695.
   [Relation d'un voyage de Paris en Limousin. English]
   Journey from Paris to the Limousin : letters to Madame de La Fontaine (1663) / Jean de La Fontaine ; translated and edited by Robert W. Berger.
      p. cm.
   Includes bibliographical references and index.
   ISBN 978-0-8386-4141-5 (alk. paper)
   1. France—Description and travel.   I. La Fontaine, Marie Héricart de. II. Berger, Robert W.   III. Title.
PQ1812.A413   2008
846'.4—dc22
                                                      2007034609

PRINTED IN THE UNITED STATES OF AMERICA

Contents

Acknowledgments	7
Introduction	11
The Letters	
Letter I	28
Letter II	31
Letter III	37
Letter IV	43
Letter V	49
Letter VI	62
Notes	69
Bibliography	88
Index	90

Acknowledgments

I WISH TO THANK MICHAEL KAUFMAN FOR HIS CRITICAL READING OF THE Introduction, and Creighton Gilbert, Thomas Hedin, and Philippe Dugimont for help in varied ways. The book is dedicated to my wife, Susan Berger, who accompanied me on a delightful trip through France, following La Fontaine's route with his Letters in hand.

Journey from Paris
to the Limousin

Introduction

CRITICS MAY ARGUE ABOUT WHO IS FRANCE'S GREATEST POET, BUT there is no question that Jean de La Fontaine (1621–95) is the most widely known. That is because his acknowledged masterpiece—the *Fables* (reworkings of those by Aesop and many others, ancient and modern)—has been translated into more languages than the poems of any of his countrymen. And these languages, in addition to the major ones of the Western world, include Arabic, Persian, Turkish, Gaelic, Creole, Hebrew, and Yiddish. The *Fables* have been translated into Occitan and into a number of French regional *patois*, such as Poitevin and Wallon; and some have even been rendered into Latin.

La Fontaine's literary immortality rests on his *Fables*, published in twelve books over a long period of time, from 1668 to 1693. But before any of the *Fables* appeared, he had published the bawdy *Contes et Nouvelles en vers* (mainly based on Boccaccio) in 1665 and 1666; a third part appeared in 1671. The poet subsequently issued *Nouveaux Contes* in 1674, others in 1682 and 1685 (a few were published posthumously).

There are other writings by La Fontaine, including, most importantly, *Les amours de Psyché et de Cupidon* (1669), a recasting of the ancient story, but still little known to the English-speaking world because it has been translated only once, in 1744. It contains some of his most exquisite verse, including descriptions of the newly created garden of Versailles. The minor writings include poems, prose pieces, plays, opera librettos, and letters, including the six travel letters that he wrote to his wife in 1663 and that are here presented in English translation for the first time. They were not published during the poet's lifetime: the first four did not appear until 1729, letters five and six in 1820, and in that same year they were all included in one volume. They have been reissued in many French editions since then, testimony to their enduring interest and charm (for their publication history see the Bibliography).

Before discussing the Letters (referred to hereafter in this form), something must be said about La Fontaine's earlier years and the circumstances surrounding his voyage from Paris to Limoges in 1663. He was born in 1621 in the town of Château-Thierry in Champagne, about fifty miles east of Paris, where his father held the post of "maître des eaux et forêts" (game and forest warden) for the duchy of Château-Thierry. He was educated there and in Paris, pursuing theological and later legal studies, and was cited as a lawyer in 1649, although he never practiced. But his real love, from his early years on, was literature, in which he immersed himself, although in an unsystematic way, aided by an excellent knowledge of Latin and some Greek. In 1647, at the age of twenty-six, he married the fourteen-year-old Marie Héricart, who provided a substantial dowry; a son was born to them in 1653. In the previous year, Jean officially inherited his father's position, which provided him with his basic income.

In 1654 La Fontaine published his first work, *L'Eunuque*, an adaptation of Terence's play *Eunuchus*, which received little attention and was never performed, as far as we know. But about 1657 he came into the orbit of Nicolas Foucquet, the royal superintendent of finances and the most enlightened art patron of the 1650s, best remembered as the builder of the dream château of Vaux-le-Vicomte, where the triumvirate who were later to create Versailles—the architect Louis Le Vau, the garden designer André Le Nôtre, and the painter Charles Le Brun—first combined their talents. La Fontaine was introduced to Foucquet by his wife's uncle, Jacques Jannart, a lawyer in the Parlement of Paris (France's highest law court), who could represent the superintendent in that body. In 1658 the poet presented Foucquet with an illuminated parchment manuscript of his lyrical poem *Adonis* (not printed until 1669). This pleased and La Fontaine was admitted in 1659 into Foucquet's circle of artists, writers, intellectuals, and aristocrats who gathered at his suburban house at Saint-Mandé, near Paris, and at Vaux. For a yearly stipend, La Fontaine was obliged to furnish Foucquet with a piece of verse each quarter, thus becoming the "official" poet to the Foucquet circle.

Of the poems written for Foucquet, the best known is *Le Songe de Vaux* (actually a mixture of prose and verse), which contains descriptions of some painted ceilings and tapestries within the château, along with an imaginary decorative scheme for the garden grotto; begun in 1659, the *Songe* was left unfinished in 1661. In Letter V to his wife, La Fontaine alluded to this work, confessing that "you know my ignorance in architectural matters, and what I said about Vaux was based only on others' reports." He had probably read the earliest writings on Vaux by Madeleine de Scudéry and André Félibien, two writers in Foucquet's little court (see Letter V, n. 1), but unlike these authors, La Fontaine's aim was to present Vaux as an ideal realm of sensuous, pagan beauty.

Le Songe remained unfinished because of the sudden fall of Foucquet in 1661. The story of his arrest, trial, and imprisonment for life is too well known to bear repetition here, but it should be pointed out that the precipitating incident—the lavish reception at Vaux of 17 August 1661, attended by Louis XIV and his court—was witnessed by La Fontaine, who described it in a letter to his friend Maucroix, then in Rome. With the arrest of the superintendent a few weeks after the *fête*, the poet's source of patronage collapsed. To make matters worse, at the end of the year La Fontaine was accused of "usurpation de noblesse" for assuming the title of "écuyer" (squire) and heavily fined in 1662.

His uncle by marriage, Jannart, suffered a worse fate. In that year, Madame Foucquet (back in Paris after having been briefly exiled to Limoges and then Saintes) wrote a series of petitions to the King, which were probably composed by Jannart. These lodged complaints against the royal agents who had confiscated the superintendent's papers; against the tribunal that was to try him; and against Jean-Baptiste Colbert, Louis XIV's minister whom she accused (correctly) of fomenting the accusations against her husband.

These petitions were ignored. Later in 1662, Foucquet, imprisoned in the Bastille and undergoing daily interrogation by the Crown-appointed "chambre de justice," demanded legal assistance, hitherto illegally denied him. One of the legal counselors he requested was Jannart, but he was rejected, although two lawyers were provided. Despite this setback, Jannart secretly went to work writing notices in defense of Foucquet, which were clandestinely published at a press set up in Montreuil-sous-Bois, in the eastern suburbs of Paris, by Madame Foucquet and her supporters.

The location of the press and Jannart's role remained hidden from the Crown, but what Colbert did uncover among the seized papers was a document, roughly drafted by Foucquet in 1657, which listed Jannart among a number of close associates who were expected to come to his aid should he ever incur the disfavor of Cardinal Mazarin, who was in control of the Regency government at that time. Furthermore, the same document revealed that some of the superintendent's properties were owned in Jannart's name—a suspicious arrangement.

In August 1663, Colbert, probably responding to Louis XIV's growing impatience with the drawn-out trial, struck. He ordered Jannart dismissed from the Parlement and sent into internal exile in Limoges. As an act of solicitude, La Fontaine offered to accompany his uncle to that distant city in the Limousin (described by Foucquet himself in his *Défenses* as "un pays rude"). Such were the circumstances which occasioned the poet's travel letters to his wife, who remained at Château-Thierry. He was now forty-two years old, without a patron, scarcely published, virtually unknown outside of a tiny circle of friends and the former members of the Foucquet circle.

Once he left Paris, La Fontaine settled into the role of tourist, observing and commenting upon people, places, and things. As his coach bumped along the roads of France, he looked out upon the changing landscape, some of which he found boring (la Beauce; Letter II), some of which moved him to impressive verse (the Loire river; Letter III). The Loire valley offered many architectural and artistic attractions: the towns of Orléans (Letter III) and Blois (Letter III), the latter pictorially described by the poet as viewed from across the Loire; the Joan of Arc monument on the bridge of Orléans (Letter II), which included one of the earliest public sculptures of the Maid (destroyed); the pilgrimage church of Notre-Dame de Cléry (Letter III), with its tomb of Louis XI ("[t]he deceiving king there pretends to be a holy man"); the château of Blois (a short course in French architectural history from the late fifteenth century to the seventeenth; Letter III), where the poet preferred the exterior of the Aile François I with its many small parts "without regularity and without order" to the wing in "modern style" (François Mansart's Aile Gaston d'Orléans, a pioneering work of the new French classicism); the château of Amboise (Letter IV), with its sad memories of Foucquet, who was briefly imprisoned there after his arrest.

But the main tourist attraction for La Fontaine was the town and château of Richelieu, south of the Loire valley in Touraine, to which he made a special excursion on horseback, accompanied by the royal officer, leaving his uncle at Châtellerault; town and château are described in his longest letter (Letter V). As he wrote to Madame de La Fontaine, it was preferable for her to know "if not the entire history of Richelieu, at least some singularities that have not escaped me." And those "singularities" which he recorded compose an entertaining, if highly selective, remembrance and critique of varied features of the architecture of town and château, the important art collection housed in the latter, and the garden, all of which he apparently regarded as a shrine to Cardinal Richelieu, to whose memory he composed a poem near the end of the Letter—"a few verses to the glory of the great Armand." Some of La Fontaine's observations about specific works of art at Richelieu will be discussed below.

In addition to his comments on landscape, architecture, and works of art, La Fontaine wrote sketches of various people whom he encountered on his trip—his traveling companions and those he met on the road and in inns or houses where he was put up. He boarded the coach at Bourg-la-Reine (Letter II): "God willed at last that the coach came by, the officer was there [the royal officer accompanying his uncle]. No monks, but in return, three women, a merchant who didn't say a word, and a notary who sang all the time and who sang very badly; he was carrying back to his region four volumes of songs. Among the three women, there was one from Poitiers who styled herself a countess."

La Fontaine goes on to paint a lively portrait of the "countess," who was in the process of separating from her husband and who related the entertaining story of Mademoiselle Barigny, a local beauty from her hometown. A Calvinist, the "countess" shows a Protestant book to the royal officer, a Catholic, and this interchange further characterizes her and brings him to life:

Monsieur de Châteauneuf (that is the officer's name) took it [the book] in hand and told her that her religion was worthless for many reasons. First, Luther had he didn't know how many bastards; the Huguenots never go to Mass; finally, he advised her to convert if she didn't want to go to Hell: for Purgatory wasn't made for people like her. The Poitevin lady immediately got out her Bible, and asked for a passage where Purgatory was spoken of.

And La Fontaine slyly adds: "During this, the notary sang all the same, Monsieur Jannart and I slept." Later the "countess" and the officer vie for the best room in an inn (Letter III).

There are descriptions of a group of gypsies under armed escort (Letter IV); of Monsieur Pidoux, his still-vital octogenarian relative in Châtellerault (Letter VI); and of two young girls, one a Pidoux in the same household, another the innkeeper's daughter in Bellac, both of whom aroused his sexual interests (Letter VI). Jannart emerges a bit from the shadows when he recounts to La Fontaine the tragicomic tale of the beggar hung by ruse at Bellac (Letter VI).

La Fontaine's *récit de voyage,* like all such writings, often imparts information about the conditions of travel and the life of its time. In 1663 travel between towns was usually by horse-drawn coach, and this entailed confinement with an often variegated and changing group of fellow travelers, as indicated in the quotation above (Letter II). There were bad roads (Letter VI), the danger of thieves (Letter II), and the occasional necessity, when the coach was laboring uphill, for the men to descend and walk alongside in order to lighten the load for the horses (Letter II). Sometimes one traveled on horseback (Letter IV), but in all cases, the indispensible work of the farrier could lead to delays (Letter VI). Coaches were very slow by modern standards, and voyagers would frequently have to be put up overnight at inns, where the sharing of beds and even drinking glasses was common (Letter III).

La Fontaine's Letters remind us of other objective facts about the France of 1663. Towns were often surrounded by walls (Letter VI), which were closed at night, preventing ingress and egress. The country then had a sizeable Protestant population, and towns like Châtellerault, the poet tells us, were equally divided between Huguenots and Catholics, the two groups having nothing to do with one another (Letter VI). And France was by no means linguistically unified at that time; "After Chauvigny," [a town near Poitiers] he wrote, "people almost no longer speak French" (Letter VI).

A modern reader of these Letters will be struck initially by the mixture of prose and verse, and this calls for comment. Being a poet, verse is a natural form of expression for La Fontaine, and he sometimes uses it to convey his deeper feelings about a subject; in this, the texture of the letters occasionally suggests the alternation of recitative and aria in opera, the former conveying the narrative action, the latter a vehicle for emotional states and reactions. The short poem in Letter IV on Foucquet's confinement at the château of Amboise is a perfect example of La Fontaine baring his deeper feelings, and the comparison with an operatic aria seems apt. But the immediate occasions which provoke the poet to verse are quite varied. One of the poems, the one about the origin of hunchbacks in the town of Orléans (Letter III), seems to have been inspired by old oral traditions and Rabelais; it gives a foretaste of the *Fables*. Other verse passages are inspired by natural features, like the one about the Loire river in the same Letter. Still others deal with the dangers and inconveniences of travel (Letters II and VI), war (Letter II), the ravages of disease upon beauty (Letter VI), and sexual desire (Letter VI); there is a satire on the town of Richelieu (Letter IV), a panegyric to the memory of Cardinal Richelieu (Letter V), and a humorous *envoi* (Letter VI) which brings some degree of closure to an epistolary series usually judged to be incomplete.

In addition to these poems, Letter V, entirely concerned with the poet's visit to the château of Richelieu, contains a number of verses on art objects: the statue of Fame atop the entrance pavilion; Michelangelo's *Slaves* (see below); and a table inlaid with gems. These continue in the venerable tradition of the verse description of works of art, premised upon the conviction that it is the elevated language of poetry that can best describe noble works of visual art. One has only to look at prior writings on the château of Richelieu itself. The earliest appeared probably in 1642, very soon after the Cardinal's death: *La description de Richelieu, à la mémoire du Cardinal-Duc* by Julien Collardeau, a poem of about eight hundred lines. In 1653 Jean Desmarets de Saint-Sorlin published *Les promenades de Richelieu, ou les vertus chrestiennes*, a small book entirely in verse, which unusually combines description with Christian moralizing (and which La Fontaine apparently carried with him on his trip). After La Fontaine's Letters, the château was again the subject of a short book of descriptive verse, Benjamin Vignier's *Le chasteau de Richelieu, ou l'Histoire des dieux et des héros de l'antiquité, avec des reflexions morales* (1676, 2nd ed. 1681). And La Fontaine himself had used verse description for a château and garden even before the Letters in *Le Songe de Vaux* (1659–61, unfinished), as noted above. This is not to say that all French seventeenth-century descriptions of works of art, architecture, and gardening were written in verse (one has only to recall André Félibien's *Description sommaire du Chasteau de Versailles* [1674], the first official guide to the palace and gardens, written entirely in prose). But verse description was a highly valued option of the time.

Finally the reader will note short verse snippets scattered throughout La Fontaine's Letters, casual jottings of his lively, poetic mind.

The Letters are suffused with classical allusions and literary references, as we might expect from a literary man who, not surprisingly, brought along some reading matter for the trip, including Livy's *History of Rome* (probably in the original; see Letter III). There are quotations and references to Virgil and Ovid among the Ancients, and among the Moderns, to the Spanish novel *Amadis de Gaula* (a French translation was available), Chapelain's unfinished poem *La Pucelle,* another Spanish novel, *Vida del Picaro Guzmán de Alfarache* (by Alemán; also available in French), a poem by Clément Marot, and a letter by Voiture. And in this connection, it is interesting to see how, in Letter III, the poet anticipates a dispute among his traveling companions about lodging in an inn by paraphrasing an amusing incident recalled from a novel by Agrippa d'Aubigné.

La Fontaine's reactions to his travel experiences are mainly of two sorts—sexual and aesthetic. The two strands come together in his contemplation of Michelangelo's *Slaves,* then standing in the château of Richelieu (now in the Louvre). After introducing them by paraphrasing what an older poet, Desmarets de Saint-Sorlin, wrote of them in 1653 ("one bears his chains patiently, the other with strength and constraint") and noting their location, he bursts into a sonnet, which reveals that to La Fontaine, a chained man signifies a lover, hard marble the coldness of women. But then the poet moves beyond these notions (which he acknowledges to be literary clichés) and considers the *Slaves* as works of art. He subscribes to the opinion that there is nothing greater than these sculptures, which surpass all modern and many ancient works. He then turns to the unfinished form at the foot of the *Dying Slave,* which scholarship recognizes to have been intended as a monkey, part of Michelangelo's complex iconography for these statues, meant as personifications of the Liberal Arts decorating the tomb of Pope Julius II. Desmarets had written of the *Dying Slave:*

> . . . ses derniers coups l'art voulut reserver,
> Deffiant l'avenir d'oser les achever.
>
> (. . . Art wanted to reserve its final strokes,
> Defying posterity to dare to finish them.)

La Fontaine expands upon these lines, to give what amounts to an early appreciation of the unfinished in art, surprising in the context of the French classical age:

> There is a passage which is as if only roughed-out: either Death, unable to tolerate the completion of a work which was to be immortal, had stopped Michelangelo at that place, or that that great person had done so intentionally, in order that posterity recognized that no one was capable of touching a figure after him. However that may be, I only esteem these two captives the more, and I maintain that the master derives as much glory from what they lack as from what he has given to them that is most finished.

In characteristic fashion, La Fontaine immediately bursts into a poetic couplet:

> May there be no complaint that the work has been found imperfect;
> Its worth is greater, its author more lamented,
>   Than if he had finished it.

At the time of La Fontaine's visit, the *Slaves* stood in niches in the stair vestibule on the ground floor. After viewing them, he was led by the concierge to the *premier étage,* where the principal paintings of Cardinal Richelieu's important collection were displayed. One of the first rooms he entered was hung with portraits of Richelieu, his family, Louis XIII, and other kings, queens, and great lords of France. But it apparently included portraits of royal mistresses, and this provoked La Fontaine to comment upon their power in history:

> In short, this cabinet is the history of our nation. They took good care not to forget the persons who have triumphed over our kings. Don't go

and imagine that I mean by that Englishmen or Spaniards; it is a much more formidable and much more powerful people of whom I wish to speak. In one word, they are the Jocondes, the Belle-Agnèses, and those illustrious conquerors, without whom Henri IV would have been an invincible prince.

"Joconde" is Mona Lisa, whom some believed to have been the mistress of François I (Leonardo's painting was in that king's collection, probably still at Fontainebleau in 1663); Belle-Agnès is Agnès Sorel (1422–50), the mistress of Charles VII.

La Fontaine's sexual approach to a work of art was appropriate for Perugino's painting, *The Combat of Love and Chastity* (now in the Louvre). He calls it "a burlesque and enigmatic combat between Pallas and Venus by a painter whom the concierge could not name for us." Actually, the central combatants are Diana (Chastity) and Venus (Love). Writing late at night from memory (his modus operandi for the Letters), the poet confesses that he would like to clearly remember the varied personages and incidents which compose the painting, and, indeed, his flawed recollections lead to a number of descriptive mistakes. La Fontaine states that Venus "wears a helmet on her head and carries a long sword," whereas in the painting she is bareheaded and carries a long flaming torch. In the left foreground Perugino had painted Minerva with helmet and cuirass, threatening a Cupid with a javelin. La Fontaine may have confused this figure with the scarcely clad Venus in the center, but it is difficult to understand how the poet, with his classical learning, could have confused the two goddesses. He then states that "Poor Venus is wounded by her enemy," but this is not so; it is true that Diana is about to launch an arrow at Venus (and from very close range), but the goddess of love has not yet been struck. But what the poet draws from his "analysis" is that by the wounding of Venus, "the artist has depicted things not as they are (for it is usually beauty that is victorious over virtue) but rather as they should be; assuredly his [i.e., the painter's] mistress had played some bad trick on him." This conclusion is curious and reveals that La Fontaine viewed the painting as an autobiographical statement by the artist, a commentary on a recent love experience. However fallacious this interpretation is, it illustrates the poet's proclivity to read sexual experience into works of art.

Continuing his tour of the château interiors, he enters one of its chapels, where he comes upon Titian's *Mary Magdalen* (actually a copy). To La Fontaine, she is a sexual object pure and simple, "fat and corpulent and very pleasant, with beautiful breasts, as in the early stages of her penitence, before the fasting had started to gain on her." He then adds parenthetically (and cryptically): "These new female penitents are dangerous, and every man of sound judgment will flee them." He follows this with only the slightest trace of shame, confessing that he has not spoken "too devoutly about the Magdalen," but that spiritual matters are not his business: "I have been in a bad state of grace my entire life."

However, not all the wonders encountered in the château lent themselves to this sort of approach. There were objects which could elicit La Fontaine's aesthetic responses and sense of wonder only. One of these was a micro-mosaic of *Saint Jerome*, which La Fontaine believed to be French, but was probably Florentine in workmanship (artist not identified). The other, also Florentine, was a huge table inlaid with precious stones—"the principal ornament of Richelieu" (now in the Galerie d'Apollon, Louvre). The table, with its enormous central agate, elicited his most extensive comments on an art object, a typical alternation of prose and verse.

As we have seen in the case of Perugino's painting, La Fontaine could be wildly off the mark in his understanding of what he was looking at. But when faced with Claude Deruet's series of the *Four Elements* (now Orléans, Musée des Beaux-Arts), he honestly confesses that "[i]f you ask me what all this means, I shall reply to you that I know nothing about it." This must have been a common experience for his contemporaries, who could rarely be expected to plumb the meaning of complex iconography, particularly, as in these instances, when the images were large in size and replete with small motifs (La Fontaine mentions the *Four Elements* as "full of little figures"). And his tour through the château, conducted by the concierge, probably was too rushed to allow the slow reading that the Deruets demand.

La Fontaine reached Limoges on 8 or 9 September; it was there that he wrote the last two Letters (V and VI), the first dated 12 September, the second 19 September. These describe the château de Richelieu and the journey from Richelieu to Limoges, concluding with a few brief, disparaging comments on the destination city.

Thus they were written several weeks after the experiences they describe.

He apparently lingered in Limoges for more than a month, in the company of Jannart (who remained there at least to the end of 1666); a document records La Fontaine back at Château-Thierry on 12 November [cited by Roger Duchêne, 1996, p. 65 n. 15 (see Bibliography)]—proof positive that his voyage was a generous act of friendship toward his uncle and had not been undertaken to fulfill some sort of abbreviated exile, as some La Fontaine scholars insist. Around this time he must have begun work on the *Contes,* the first of which, "Joconde," was granted a *privilège du roi* on 14 January 1664, but not published until the following year in the first volume of the *Contes et Nouvelles en vers.* The first book of the *Fables* appeared three years later, vaulting the poet from obscurity to immediate literary fame.

There is nothing remarkable about a man, while traveling on the road, writing letters to his wife back home. But in the case of La Fontaine, his occasional disparaging comments addressed to her, as well as his frank revelations about his sexual desires, pique our curiosity about their relationship. Marie Héricart, from a good family of Ferté-Milon, near Château-Thierry, was fourteen and a half when she married La Fontaine in 1647, but that was about the age when most girls in seventeenth-century France got married. According to the gossipy Tallemant des Réaux, the poet was unfaithful to her, and it is possible that Marie responded in kind. Around 1658, five years after the birth of their son, the couple obtained a legal separation of their worldly goods, but this did not affect their marital status. They continued to live together in his ancestral home at Château-Thierry, although he traveled frequently and alone to Paris, Vaux, and Reims. Only later, around 1671/72, did the couple begin to separate; much, much later, in 1693, the elderly pair was reunited.

What, then, are we to make of La Fontaine's sometimes rude and often insensitive remarks in his letters to Marie? In the very first paragraph of Letter I, he pours forth a series of reproaches: "You do not engage in amusements, or work, or trouble yourself with housekeeping; and, aside from the time that your good friends give you out of charity, you only divert yourself by reading novels. This is a stock soon used up."

The poet proposes a new genre of reading for her, namely "history, either of places or persons," a genre which his travel letters will introduce her to. For then: "You would have the wherewithal with which to divert yourself your whole life, provided that this was without the intention of remembering anything, still less of citing anything. It is not a good quality in a woman to be learned, and it is a very bad one to affect appearing as such."

La Fontaine here anticipates a passage in Molière's *Les Femmes Savantes* of 1672, but the sentiment was a common one among seventeenth-century French males, although it utterly failed to halt the rise into intellectual and artistic prominence of figures such as Madame de La Fayette and Madame de Sévigné.

However that may be, the whole series of letters could hardly have been a comfort to Madame de La Fontaine as far as her marriage was concerned. Again in the first Letter, he looks forward to seeing the women of the Limousin region "of the highest bourgeoisie" who wear, he has been told, "hoods of sharp-pink cloth over caps of black velvet"—a remarkable detail of costume because such caps were usually worn by very low-class women. But then he adds: "If I find one of these hoods covering a pretty head, I will be able to amuse myself in passing, but only through curiosity." In Letter II, when speaking of the "countess," one of his fellow coach travelers, he writes that "I might have found a motive for flattering her, if I had also found her beautiful; but without that, nothing touches me"—comforting words, perhaps, for Marie (a good-looking woman, to judge from contemporary depictions), but disconcerting in another sense. In Letter V, in his introduction to his long description of the château de Richelieu, La Fontaine again reminds his wife of her lack of learning: "Knowing your turn of mind, a gallantry about these matters [i.e. the château and its history] will please you more than so many learned and particular observations." And what did Marie think about Jean's revelations in Letter VI, when he spoke frankly about his attraction to his adolescent relative in Châtellerault, "whom I gladly gazed upon," adding that "I was quite resolved, if we had stayed longer at Châtellerault, to turn her over on as many sides until I would have discovered what was in her soul, and if she is capable of a secret passion." And then the innkeeper's daughter at Bellac (also Letter VI), "a young and rather pretty person," with whom he flirted even though she didn't speak French:

> but that person understood me without much difficulty; gallant speech is understood in all lands, and has this convenience in that it carries with it its interpreter. However sorry our quarters were, I did not fail to spend a very pleasant night there; my sleep was in no way chequered with dreams, as it usually is. If however Morpheus had led the host's daughter to me, I certainly think I would not have turned her away; he didn't do so and I did without her.

Perhaps, as Ange-Marie Caudal has suggested, La Fontaine expressed his real desire about his marital relationship in the conclusion of the story of that Poitevin beauty, La Barigny (Letter II):

> There is, it is said, a sacrament of marriage between them [La Barigny and her last lover], but the matter is kept secret. What do you say about these marriages of conscience? Those who have introduced the practice were not foolish; one is a girl and a wife all at once; the husband acts like a suitor: as long as the affair remains in that state, there is no reason to oppose it. The parents don't make a big fuss, everything comes about in its course, and if it happens that they tire of one another, they don't have to go to a judge or a bishop.

These comments of La Fontaine, addressed to his wife, may betoken the state of their relationship in 1663: a wife who was used to intellectual belittlement, a husband whose philandering was open and tolerated by her. However that may be, the fact that the Letters contain such passages is surely of importance in weighing the validity of an argument that has developed within French literary criticism: that the Letters were not simply composed for the private consumption of his wife, but also for circulation within Madame de La Fontaine's private circle (the "Académie de Château-Thierry," a sort of literary club), and with eventual publication in mind.

That letters were often passed around or read aloud to a group in seventeenth-century France is known from Madame de Sévigné's correspondence. For example, on 9 September 1694, while staying with her daughter and her family at Grignan, she replied to a letter from her relative, Monsieur de Coulanges: "I have received your many letters, my dear cousin; none of them has been lost. It would have been a terrible shame if they had: each has its special merit and, all together, they constitute the delight of our society."

But, the modern reader is justified in asking, would Madame de La Fontaine have shared those of the Letters with the embarrassing passages cited above? How could their author have expected her to do so? And if the very first of the series started off on so pejorative a note, as we have seen, would not this have been an opening signal that the entire correspondence was meant for her alone? It is true that at the beginning of Letter V, in introducing his description of Richelieu, he wrote that "[t]hose who will look for these learned observations in my letters to you will be making a big mistake," but this can simply be understood as a rhetorical turn of phrase.

Only two of the Letters (V and VI) survive as autograph manuscripts (Paris, Bibliothèque de l'Arsenal). Letter VI has very few changes, but Letter V, containing the long description of the château of Richelieu, has frequent crossings-out and emendations. Differences in ink color could suggest ulterior editing in later years, but an examination of the ink under magnification indicates that it was unstable, with shifts in color from brown to black even within unaltered words. The changes in this Letter and the variations in the ink can be understood as dating from the same evening (12 September 1663) when La Fontaine set pen to paper.

There is no evidence whatsoever that, in subsequent years, the poet attempted, or even thought, to publish the set (along with any others that may have been lost, subsequent to his arrival at Limoges). There can be little doubt that La Fontaine's Letters to his wife were meant as private missives for her alone, and not to be shared with others, let alone with posterity. And that is the intention and fate of almost all letters ever written.

A half-century ago, the literary historian Philip A. Wadsworth remarked (in *Young La Fontaine* [1952]):

> His letters . . . have exact prototypes in the epistles in prose and verse which La Fontaine and other authors were exchanging in the 1650s and 1660s. From the "Relation d'une fête donnée à Vaux," composed for Maucroix, it is only a step to the *Voyage en Limousin*. An even closer model, because of the similar subject-matter, can be found in Racine's first letter from Uzès, in 1661, where he recounts to La Fontaine—

gracefully, urbanely, rather eruditely—his impressions of the Rhône, of the language of Provence, and of the beautiful women he has seen.

It is worth examining these two letters—one composed by La Fontaine, the other addressed to him by his distant relative, Jean Racine (the future great dramatist)—because, as Wordsworth indicates, they provide precedents for those that compose the epistolary series of 1663.

Already in La Fontaine's letter to Maucroix of 22 August 1661, there is the lively mixture of prose and verse that we find in the Letters to his wife; one of the poems, celebrating the fireworks which brought the festivities at Vaux to a conclusion, occupies forty-six short lines. But Racine's letter to La Fontaine, written from Uzès on 11 November of the same year, not only contains some lines of verse amid the prose, but is the record of a traveler's impressions, with that touch of humor and good cheer that was to characterize the *Voyage de Paris en Limousin*. In the following excerpt, Racine's group is traveling from Paris to Lyon not by coach but on horseback; later he continues on by boat down the Rhône river to reach Uzès, a common avenue of transportation in a country rich in navigable rivers:

> We have had only two hours of rain from Paris to Lyon. Our company was jovial, and rather pleasant. There were three Huguenots, an Englishman, two Italians, a counsellor of the Châtelet, two secretaries of the King, and two of his musketeers. At last, we were nine or ten in number. I didn't fail every evening to break into a gallop before the others in order to go reserve my bed; . . . Thus I was always well-bedded; and when I arrived in Lyon, I didn't feel any more tired than if I had gone from the Sainte-Geneviève quarter to that of the Rue Galande [in Paris].
>
> In Lyon I only remained two days with two musketeers of our group who were from Pont Saint-Esprit. Eight days ago we embarked on a very new and well-protected vessel that we expressly reserved from the best owner in the region. For it is not too much precaution to set course upon the Rhône with guarantees. Nevertheless, since it hadn't rained at all going towards Lyon, the Rhône was very low, and had lost much of its usual swiftness.
>
> > One could without difficulty
> > See its Naiads entirely naked,

> And who, ashamed of being seen,
> In order to hide their nudity
> Sought out unknown places.
> These Nymphs are large rocks,
> Authors of many sepulchres,
> And whose frightful forms
> Cause the faces of the most daring pilots to change.

We were two days on the Rhône, and we slept at Vienne and at Valence. After Lyon I scarcely began to understand the language of the country any more, and to be no longer intelligible myself. This adversity increased at Valence, and God willed that having asked a servant for a chamber-pot, she set a chafing-dish under my bed. You can imagine the results of this wretched adventure, and what can happen to a drowsy man who makes use of a chafing-dish for his night-time necessities. (Translated from Jean Racine, *Lettres d'Uzès,* ed. Jean Dubu [Uzès: Ateliers Henri Peladan, 1963], 2–3.)

Racine goes on to say that he needed an interpreter as badly as would a Muscovite in Paris, and relates the amusing incident of how his request for carpet tacks was misunderstood for matches (see Letter VI, n16).

These letters (one written by La Fontaine, the other addressed to him) prove that by 1663 the poet was using or was acquainted with the literary style that we find in his Letters to his wife. By that time, this epistolary mode, applied to a *récit de voyage,* flowed spontaneously from his pen. Never intended for the public, the *Voyage de Paris en Limousin* has, since its complete publication in the early nineteenth century, won the hearts of readers of French as one of the earliest truly personal travel accounts in that language, and the great poet's most intimate revelation of his mind and personality.

Letter I

YOU HAVE NEVER WANTED TO READ ABOUT TRAVELS OTHER THAN THOSE of the Knights of the Round Table, but ours well deserve your reading. Yet you will encounter material little suited to your taste. It is for me to make it palatable, if I can, in such a manner that it pleases you; and it is for you to praise my intention, even though not followed by success. It may even happen, if you enjoy this account, that you will afterward enjoy more serious matter. You do not engage in amusements,[1] or work, or trouble yourself with housekeeping; and, aside from the time that your good friends give you out of charity, you only divert yourself by reading novels.[2] This is a stock soon used up. You have read the old ones so many times that you know them by heart; few new ones are written; and among these few, all are not good; thus you often remain as in a drought. Consider, if you please, how useful this would be for you, if, in fun, I had accustomed you to history, either of places or persons. You would have the wherewithal with which to divert yourself your whole life, provided that this was without the intention of remembering anything, still less of citing anything. It is not a good quality in a woman to be learned, and it is a very bad one to affect appearing as such.[3]

We departed Paris then on the 23rd of the present month [August 1663], after Monsieur Jannart had received condolences from a great many persons of quality and from his friends.[4] Monsieur le lieutenant-criminel[5] treated generously, liberally, royally; he opened his purse and told us that we had only to reach in; the rest of the neighborhood performed wonders. Even if it had been a question of transferring the Quai des Orfèvres, the courtyard of the Palais, and the Palais itself to Limoges, the matter would not have happened otherwise.[6] Finally, there were at our house only processions of crestfallen and thunderstruck people. With all that, I did not weep; that led me to believe that I shall acquire a great reputation for steadfastness in this affair.

The fancy of traveling had entered my mind some time before, as if I had had presentiments of the king's order. It had been more than a fortnight since I spoke of nothing else, than to go soon to Saint-Cloud, soon to Charonne, and I was ashamed of having lived so long without seeing anything. I shall no longer be reproached for that, thank heavens! We were told, among other marvels, that many of the Limousin women of the highest bourgeoisie wear hoods of sharp-pink cloth over caps of black velvet. If I find one of these hoods covering a pretty head, I will be able to amuse myself in passing, but only through curiosity.

Be that as it may, I have an entirely good opinion of our journey. We have already done three leagues without any bad accident, except that Monsieur Jannart's sword broke; but since we are people who profit from all our misfortunes, we also found that, indeed, it was too long and inconvenient for him. Now we are at Clamart, beneath that famous mountain where Meudon is situated; there we are going to rest ourselves for two or three days. In truth, traveling is a pleasure, you always encounter something remarkable. You cannot believe how excellent is the butter that we eat. I wished for myself twenty times over some such cows, a similar meadow, the same waters and the rest of it, except for the butter churner, who is a bit old.

The garden of Madame C . . . also deserves to have a place in this story; it has many very rustic places, and that is what I love above all. Either you have seen it or you haven't seen it; if you have seen it, do you remember those two terraces facing the parterre and at the left, and the rows of oak and chestnut trees which border them? I am very much mistaken if that isn't beautiful. Do you also remember that wood that appears in the background, with the blackness of a forest aged by ten centuries? The trees in truth are not so old, but all the same they can pass for the oldest in the village; and I don't believe there are more venerable ones on earth. The two avenues which are to the right and left still please me. They have that particularity, in that that which confines them is that which makes them appear more beautiful. That on the right has quite the appearance of a tennis court. It is presently bordered by an amphitheater of grass, and the rear is raised up by eight or ten steps; it gives the appearance that it is the place where the local divinities receive the homage due them.

If the god Pan, or Faunus,
Prince of the wood, it is said,
Ever has a throne set up,
That will be the model.

Two chestnut-trees, whose shade
Is majestic and cool,
Cover it with their foliage,
In the same way as a rich canopy.

I see nothing that equals it,
Nor that charms me to my liking,
Like a lawn that spreads out
All along each step.

I prefer this grass a hundred times more
Than the precious carpet
On which the proud Orient
Sees its emperors seated.

Simple and divine beauties,
You satisfied our ancestors,
Before they removed from the mines
That which strikes our eyes.

For what does so much expense serve?
The great ones praise themselves in vain;
Long live magnificence
Which costs only the planting.

These moralities notwithstanding, I advised Madame C . . . to have a house built, proportioned in some way to the beauty of her garden, and to ruin herself by this. We shall depart from her place, and at Bourg-la-Reine we are going to take the convenience of the Poitiers coach, which passes here every Sunday. A king's officer is to be found there, who is under order to accompany us as far as Limoges. I will write to you about what happens to us on the road, and what seems to me worthy of observation. In the meantime, do give my compliments to our little monkey,[7] and tell him that perhaps I shall bring back from that land some pretty little governess to play with and to keep him company.

At Clamart, 25 August 1663.

Letter II

THE OCCUPATIONS THAT WE HAD AT CLAMART, YOUR UNCLE AND I, WERE different. He didn't do anything worth remembering. He diverted himself with preparing legal papers, briefs, and other matters. This wasn't the case with me; I walked, I slept, I spent time with the ladies who came to see us.

Sunday having arrived, we left very early in the morning. Madame C . . . and our aunt[1] accompanied us as far as Bourg-la-Reine. We waited there almost three hours; and in order to dissipate our boredom, or to bore us even more (I don't really know which I should say), we heard Mass at a parish church. The procession, the holy water, the homily, nothing was lacking. As good luck would have it, the parish priest was ignorant, and didn't preach. God willed at last that the coach came by, the officer was there. No monks, but in return, three women, a merchant who didn't say a word, and a notary who sang all the time and who sang very badly; he was carrying back to his region four volumes of songs. Among the three women, there was one from Poitiers who styled herself a countess; she seemed rather young, and of moderate height, gave evidence of being intelligent, disguised her name, and had just gone to law to be separated from her husband, all qualities of good omen. And I might have found a motive for flattering her, if I had also found her beautiful; but without that, nothing touches me, and in my opinion that's the main point. I challenge you to have me find a grain of salt in a person who lacks it [beauty]. Such therefore was the company that we had until Port-de-Piles.

It was necessary at last that uncle and aunt separated; the last good-byes were tender, and would have been much more so, if the coachman had given us the leisure to complete them. Since he wanted to regain the time that he had lost, he drove us at first with dispatch. Upon going out of Bourg-la-Reine, one leaves Sceaux on the right and, at several leagues from there, Chilly[-Mazarin] on the left, then Montlhéry on the same side. Does one say Montlhéry or

Montlehéry? It's Montlehéry when the verse is too short, and Montlhéry when it's too long.² Montlhéry therefore or Montlehéry, as you wish, was a fortress of old, which the English, when they were masters of France, built on a rather high hill.³ At the foot of that hill is a market town that has kept the name. As for the fortress, it is demolished, but not by the years; that which remains, which is a very high tower, has not fallen into ruin, although they destroyed one side of it. There is still a stair remaining, and two rooms where English paintings[4] are seen, which is proof of the antiquity and singularity of the place. Such is what I learned from your uncle, who says that he entered the rooms; as for me, I saw nothing. The coachman only wanted to stop at Châtres [now Arpajon], a little town belonging to Monsieur de Candé,[5] one of our great forest wardens.

We dined there. After the meal, we again saw many châteaux on the right and left; I didn't say a word, it would have been an infinite labor. But we passed near Plessis-Pâté,[6] and then traversed the valley of Cocatrix, after having ascended that of Torfou: for even without having studied philosophy, you can imagine that there is no valley without a mountain. I do not think about that valley of Torfou without shuddering.

> It is a dangerous passage,
> A place for thieves, ambush, and lairs,[7]
> A wood on the left, a mountain on the right,
>   Between the two
>   An empty road.
> The mountain is all full
> Of rocks fashioned like those
> Of our little domain.[8]

Whatever men there were in the coach, we descended in order to relieve the horses.[9] For as long as the road continued, I didn't talk about anything else but the advantages of war. Indeed, if it produces thieves, it keeps them busy, which is a great benefit for everyone, and especially for me, who naturally fears encountering them. They say that this wood which we skirted swarms with them; that's not good, it deserved to be burnt down.

> Republic of wolves, sanctuary of brigands,
>   Must you exist in the world?

> You favor the wicked,
>   By your thick and deep shade.
> They slit the throat of the one whom Themis,[10] or profit,
> Or the desire to see, causes to leave his soil![11]
> In how many ways, alas, does mankind
>   Make war upon itself!
> May heaven's fire desolate its precincts!
> May the fire of love never make itself felt there
>   Nor be cooled there!
> Instead of Amarillis, Diana, and Aminta,
> Only wretched woodcutters are found among you,
>   Charcoal-sellers, black like demons,
>   Who suit you in such a way
>   That you are to all the thieves
>   What is called a cemetery.

Our first stage of the journey ended later than the others; however, there remained enough daylight for us to notice, upon entering Étampes, some vestiges of our wars [of the Fronde]. They were not the richest that I have seen. I found there much in Gothic style; there was certainly the work of Mars, worthless mason if ever there was one.

> He leaves us these monuments,
> In order to mark some of our troubles.
> When Turenne laid siege to Tavannes,
> Turenne did what the court told him;
> Tavannes, no, for he defended himself,
> And blew on a pea-shooter.[12]
>
> Much French blood was then spilled;
> Both sides lost in the civil war.
>   Our prince had always lost,
>   Even when he had won a city.

Finally, we beheld with pity the suburbs of Étampes. Picture a series of houses without roofs, without windows, pierced through on all sides; nothing is uglier and more hideous. That recalled to my mind the ruins of great Troy. Truly, Fortune indeed laughs at the work of man. I conversed with our group in the evening. The next day we passed through the Beauce, a boring region, and which (besides the inclination I have to sleep) furnished us with a very fine subject. To refrain from that [i.e., sleeping], a question of religious controversy was brought forward: our countess was the cause of this. She is Calvinist and showed us a book by du Moulin.[13] Monsieur de Châteauneuf (that is the officer's name) took it in hand and told her that her religion was worthless for many reasons. First, Luther had he didn't know how many bastards; the Huguenots never go to Mass; finally, he advised her to convert if she didn't want to go to Hell: for Purgatory wasn't made for people like her. The Poitevin lady immediately got out her Bible, and asked for a passage where Purgatory was spoken of. During this, the notary sang all the same, Monsieur Jannart and I slept.

In the afternoon, fearing that Monsieur de Châteauneuf would bring controversy back upon us, I asked our unknown countess if there were beautiful persons in Poitiers. She named several for us, among whom a girl named Barigny, of modest circumstances, for her father was only a tailor; but in other respects one couldn't say enough about the beauty of that person. She had light-brown hair, a beautiful figure, an admirable bosom, just the right amount of plumpness, all facial features well made, beautiful eyes; so that, on the whole, there was little more to wish for, for nothing was too much to say. Finally, not only the provincial stars, but those of the court had to yield to her, to the point that at a ball where the king was present, as soon as la Barigny entered, she effaced whatever glittered; the greatest suns appeared in comparison only as simple stars. Besides that, she had read novels and was not lacking in wit. As for her behavior, she was considered in Poitiers to be an honest girl within the limits of a "marriage of conscience" [a marriage to regularize an illicit situation]. Formerly a gentleman, called Miravaux, had been passionately in love with her, and wanted to marry her by all means. The gentleman's parents were opposed to this; they might however have gained nothing if Clotho[14] had not gotten involved in the business; the lover died while in the army, in which he commanded a regiment. The last actions of his life and his last sighs were only for his mistress. He left her twelve thousand *écus* in his will, besides a quantity of furniture and small objects of importance which he had given to her previously. Upon hearing of this death, Mademoiselle Barigny said the most pitiful things in the world, affirmed that she would allow herself to die now or later, and in the meantime collected the legacy that her lover had left her. Lawsuit for that at the tribunal in Poitiers, appeal to the court: but who would not prefer a beautiful woman to the heirs? The judges did what I would have done. The woman's heart was contested for with yet more passion. It was one Cartignon by name who inherited it. This last lover proved to be luckier than the other: the beauty took care that he not die without being paid for his labors. There is, it is said, a sacrament of marriage between them, but the matter is kept secret. What do you say about these marriages of conscience? Those who have introduced the practice were not foolish; one is a girl and a wife all at once; the husband acts like a suitor: as long as the affair remains in that state, there is no reason to oppose it. The parents don't make a big fuss, everything comes about in its course, and if it happens that they tire of one another, they don't have to go to a judge or a bishop. There you have the story of la Barigny.

These adventures diverted us to such a degree that we entered Orléans almost without noticing it. It even seemed that the sun was as amused to hear them as we, for although we had made twenty leagues, it wasn't yet at the end of its journey. Besides, whether la Barigny was that evening out walking, whether it was to set in the bosom of some charming river like the Loire, it was so bedecked, that Monsieur de Châteauneuf and I went to gaze at it from the bridge. At the same place I saw the Pucelle [a statue of Joan of Arc], but really it was without pleasure: I found in her neither the appearance, the stature, nor the face of an Amazon.[15] The Infanta Gradafillée[16] is worth ten like her, and if it wasn't that Monsieur Chapelain[17] is her chronicler, I don't know if I would mention it. I gazed at it out of my affection for him longer than I would have. She is kneeling before a cross, and king Charles [VII] is in the same posture opposite her; the entire thing is extremely poor and of trifling appearance. It is a monument in which the poverty of its century is perceptible.

The bridge of Orléans did not appear to me either of a width or of a majesty proportioned to the nobility of its use and to the place that it occupies in the universe.

> It is not a small glory
> To be a bridge over the Loire.
> It sees pass at its feet
> The most beautiful of rivers.
> How many of its vast courses
> Phoebus sees flowing!

It is nearly three times wider at Orléans than the Seine is at Paris. The horizon, very beautiful on all sides, and bounded as it should be; so that that river being shallow in comparison, its waters very clear, its course without meanders, one would say that it is a canal. From both sides of the bridge one continually sees boats passing under sail; some go upstream, others downstream; and since the bank is not as large as in Paris, nothing hinders seeing all of them clearly. One counts them, one notices how far one is from the other, it is what composes one of its beauties; indeed, it would be a pity if water so pure were entirely covered by boats. Their sails are very ample; that imparts to them a shiplike majesty, and I imagined myself seeing the port of Constantinople in little. Moreover, Orléans, viewed from the Sologne, is of a beautiful appearance. Since the town spreads uphill, one perceives almost all of it. The mall and the other trees that have been planted in many places all along the rampart make it appear half-closed in by green walls, and in my opinion that becomes it well. I would bore you to give details about what's inside: there is already too much for you about this subject. You shall know however that the quarter by which we went down to the bridge is very ugly, the remainder rather beautiful, with spacious, clean, pleasant streets, which testify to their good city. I didn't have enough time to see the rampart, but I allowed myself to be told a lot of good things about it, as well as about the church of Sainte-Croix.

Finally our group, which had dispersed this way and that, returned satisfied. One spoke about one thing, the other about something else. Supper time having arrived, knights and ladies were seated at their rather poorly spread tables, afterward went to bed immediately, as one might imagine; and with that, the chronicler brings the present chapter to a close.

At Amboise, 30 August 1663.

Letter III

As much as the Beauce had seemed boring to me, so much did the countryside between Orléans and Amboise appear pleasant and diverting. At the start we had the Sologne, a province less fertile than the Vendômois, which is on the other side of the river. Also one gets a simpleton of the region for very little, for these are not crazy like those of Champagne or Picardy. I believe that the female simpletons cost more.[1]

The first place we halted was Cléry. I went right away to visit the church: it is a collegiate church rather well endowed for a village, not that the canons agree about that, or that I heard them say so. Louis XI is buried here: one sees him kneeling on his tomb, four children at the corners: they would be four angels, and might be four putti, if their wings hadn't been pulled out.[2] The deceiving king there pretends to be a holy man, and looks much better than when the Burgundian led him to Liège.[3]

> I found in him the look of a sly dog;
> So was that prince, whose life
> Should rarely serve as an example to kings,
> Even if it might be followed in a few cases.

At his knees are his book of hours and his rosary, and other little implements, his hand of justice, his scepter, his hat, and his statuette of Our Lady. I don't know how the sculptor did not include the provost Tristan.[4] The whole is of white marble, and seemed to me of a rather good hand.

Upon leaving that church, I mistook another inn for ours. I very nearly ordered dinner, and having gone to walk in the garden, I became so interested in reading Livy, that more than a good hour went by without my giving thought to my appetite. A servant from that house having informed me of that error, I ran to the place where we had gotten off, and I arrived in sufficient time to be included.

From Cléry to Saint-Dyé-sur-Loire, which is the usual halting place, there are only four leagues; the road is pleasant and bordered by hedgerows, which led me to take part of the stretch on foot. No adventure worth recording happened to me, except that I encountered, it seems to me, two or three tramps and some pilgrims of Saint James. Since Saint-Dyé is only a village with poorly furnished inns, and our countess not being satisfied with her room, and Monsieur de Châteauneuf always wanting your uncle to be the best lodged, we expected to fall into a dispute between Potrot and the lady from Nouaillé.[5] The servants of Potrot and those of the lady from Nouaillé, having placed, during the fair of Niort, the clothes of their master and of their mistress in the same inn and on the same bed, that created a dispute. Potrot said: "I will sleep in that bed there." "I do not say that you will not sleep in it," answered the lady from Nouaillé, "but I will sleep in it also." Upon point of honor and in order not to yield, they both slept there. The matter happened in another way: the next day the countess complained very much about fleas. I don't know if it was that which awakened the coachman (I mean the fleas of the coachman, and not those of the countess). At all events, it caused us to leave so very early, that it was scarce 8:00 a.m. when we found ourselves opposite Blois, with nothing but the Loire between.

Blois is on a slope, like Orléans, but is smaller and denser; the roofs of houses are disposed in many places in such a way that they resemble the stairs in an amphitheater. That appeared very beautiful to me, and I believe that one could only with difficulty find a view more pleasing and more agreeable. The château is at one end of the town, at the other end is Saint-Solenne;[6] that church appears very large and isn't hidden by any houses; in brief, it makes a fine pendant to the prince's dwelling. Each of these buildings is sited on an eminence, whose slopes join toward the center of town, so that Blois very nearly forms a crescent, of which Saint-Solenne and the château form the horns. I did not inquire about their old customs. As for the present, the way of life here is very refined: either that it has always been that way and that the climate and the beauty of the countryside contributed to it, or that the residence of Monsieur [Gaston d'Orléans] has introduced that politeness or the number of pretty women. I introduced myself to some of them, as I usually do. Besides that, people wanted to show me some hunchbacks, a rather common thing in Blois, according to what they told me, but still more common in Orléans. I believed that heaven, the friend of these people, sent some wit to them by that means, for they say that a hunchback never lacks any; and yet there are some old traditions that give another reason for it. Here is what they taught me: it concerns also the situation of the Beauce[7] and the Limousin.

> The Beauce formerly had hills in abundance,
> > Like the rest of France.
> > About which the town of Orléans
> Full of happy, delicate, idle people,
> > Who wanted to walk in comfort,
> > Complained, and threatened to make trouble,
> > And messieurs the men of Orléans
> > Said to Fate all in one voice,
> > Once, twice, thrice,
> > That it was obliged to remove from them the difficulty
> Of climbing, descending, and climbing back again.
> > "What! Always hill and never plain!
> > Give us triple breath,
> > Legs of iron, strong disposition,
> > Or give us a land
> > That no longer has hill or mountain."
> > "Oh! oh!" Fate replied to them,
> "You cause mutinies, and in all of Gaul
> I see only you alone who complain about hills.
> > Since they harm your feet,
> > You shall have them on your shoulders."
> > Then the Beauce to level out,
> > To make even, to become
> > A land smooth as ice;
> > And hunchbacks to be born in the locality,
> > And hills to remove from the land.
> > All of them could not be placed upon the people,
> > So that the celestial troop,
> > Not knowing what to do with the remainder,
> Was on the point of placing them on the neighboring land,
> When Jupiter said: "Let us spare the Touraine
> > And the Blésois, for this domain
> > Will one day belong to my kin.[8]
> > Let us put them in the Limousin."[9]

Those of Blois, as neighbors and good friends of those of Orléans, have relieved them of a part of their loads. Both will yet have a generation of hunchbacks, and then that's the end of it.

You will have for that tradition such conviction as will please you; what I assure you to be very true is that Monsieur de Châteauneuf and I took lunch very nicely, and afterward went to see the prince's dwelling.[10] It was built in several stages, one part under François I, the other under one of his predecessors: facing one is a main building in modern style, that late Monsieur [Gaston d'Orléans] had work started on. All these three parts compose, thank goodness, no symmetry, and have no relationship nor fitness one with the other; the architect avoided that as much as he could. The part built by François I, viewed from the exterior, pleased me more than all the rest. There are a great many little galleries, little windows, little balconies, little ornaments without regularity and without order; that makes for something grand which rather pleases. We didn't have the leisure to see the interior. I only regretted [not seeing] the bedroom where Monsieur died, for I had considered it to be a relic; indeed, there is no one who must not have an extreme veneration for the memory of that prince. The peoples of these regions mourned him with reason still. Never was a reign more gentle, more tranquil, nor happier than his had been;[11] and in truth princes like this should be born a little more often, or not die. I also had very much desired to see his garden of plants, which, during his lifetime, was considered the most perfect in the world:[12] it did not please our coachman, who only cared about taking an ample lunch, so he made us leave.

As long as the journey lasted, we had fine weather, a fine road, fine countryside; especially did the embankment not leave us or we did not leave the embankment, one is the same as the other. It is a causeway that follows the banks of the Loire, and holds back that river in its bed: a work that has cost much time to make, and that costs yet more to maintain. As for the countryside, I cannot tell you enough of its marvels. None of those bald mountains that shock our dear Monsieur de Maucroix[13] so much; but on one side and the other, low hills covered in the most pleasing manner in the world. You will hear me speak of them more than once, but while waiting,

> What say we what the Loire was
> Before being what it is?
> For you know that concerning its history
> Our good Ovid is silent.

LETTER III

Was it some pleasing person,
Some queen, some Amazon,
Some nymph in the depth of a rock,
Whom no lover knew how to reach?
Its origins are common,
That is why let us not look for
The Jupiters and Neptunes,
Or the gods Pan who pursued
All the beauties whom they found.
Let us leave aside those metamorphoses,
And let us say here, if you please,
That the Loire was what it is
Since the beginning of things.

The Loire is therefore a river
Flowing through a countryside favored by the heavens,
Gentle when it so pleases, when it so pleases so bold,
That its imperious course is scarcely halted.
It would ravage a thousand fertile harvests,
Engulf villages, cause towns to float,
    Destroy everything in one night;
    It would take only one day
    To see it carry away the fruit
    Of an entire year's labor,
If along its banks there wasn't a levee,
    That they carefully maintain.
    From the moment that a place gives way,
    It is restored right away;
    The least breach doesn't remain without it being
      corrected immediately.
    And for that maintenance,
    The only obstacle to such ravages,
    Each has its assessment,
    Communities, market-towns, and villages.

You may well believe that, being on its banks,
Our people and I did not fail
    To turn our eyes all around.
    I experienced such delightful attractions,
    That my heart is still deeply moved.
    Low pleasant hills are on both sides,
    Low hills not so close to the clouds
    As in the Limousin, but low enchanted hills,

Fine houses, beautiful and well-planted parks,
Verdant meadows, in which this countryside abounds,
Vineyards and woods, so many diverse things,
That one at first believes oneself to be in another world.

But the most beautiful object without doubt is the Loire:
One rarely sees it straying from its path,
It has few meanders in its measured course,
It isn't a stream which winds in a meadow:
    She is the daughter of Amphitrite;
    She it is whose merit,
    Name, glory, and shores
  Are worthy of these provinces,
Whom our princes have always placed
    Among all their greatest treasures.
    She spreads her crystal waters
      With magnificence,
And the garden of France
    Deserved such a channel.

    I am angry with her for one thing, which is, having seen her, I imagined that there was nothing more to see; I had neither curiosity nor desire. Richelieu certainly changed my opinion.

    This Richelieu is certainly an admirable object: I dated my third letter from there because that is where I finished it. See how you are beholden to me, it is a quarter of an hour before midnight, and we must get up tomorrow before the sun, although it had promised when setting that it would rise up very early in the morning. Yet I use the hours that are the most precious to me to make reports to you, I who am the child of sleep and laziness. Let them speak to me after this about husbands who sacrificed themselves for their wives: I claim to surpass them all, and you cannot acquit yourself toward me unless you wish me as many good nights as the bad ones that I shall have before our trip is over.

                        At Richelieu, 3 September 1663.

Letter IV

We arrived at Amboise rather early, but in very bad weather. I did not omit using the remainder of the day to see the château.[1] I will not amuse myself drawing up the plan for you, and for a very good reason: you will know nothing more than toward the town it is situated on a rock, and appears extremely high. Toward the countryside the surrounding ground is more elevated. Within the precincts there are three or four very remarkable things. The first are those stag's horns so much talked about, and about which they don't talk enough, in my opinion; for whether one may choose to have it pass for natural or artificial, I find it almost equally an object of astonishment. Those who find it artificial come to an agreement that they are stag's horns, but of several pieces; now the way they have joined them without the appearance of connections [remainder of sentence lost]. To also say that they are natural and that the universe may have at some time produced an animal sufficiently large to carry them, that is hardly believable.[2]

> It will always be doubted,
> Even if that stag would have been
> Older than a patriarch.
> Such an animal, in truth,
> Could never have been contained in the Ark.

That which I also noticed as curious were two towers built of earth like wells.[3] Within they built stairs in the form of ramps, by which you descend to the foot of the château, so that they reach down, in the same way as the oaks of which Virgil speaks,

> With one end in the heavens, the other in the underworld.[4]

I found them well built, and their structure pleased me as much as the rest of the château appeared to us unworthy of detaining us. Nevertheless there was a time when it served as a cradle for our young kings,[5] and truly it was a cradle built of quite solid materials, and which was not to be easily destroyed. That which is beautiful is the view: it is grand, majestic, of immense scope; the eye finds nothing to block it; no object that does not occupy it in the most pleasant way in the world. One imagines espying Tours, although it is fifteen or twenty leagues away [*recte:* six]. Moreover, one has in view the most pleasant and best diversified hills I ever saw, and at the foot [of the château] a grassland which the Loire flows through, for that river passes at Amboise.

All of this poor Monsieur Foucquet[6] could never, during his stay, enjoy for a single moment; they had closed up all the windows of his room, leaving only a hole up above. I asked to see it (sad pleasure), I confess it to you, but finally I demanded it. The soldier who led us didn't have the key; lacking that, I spent a long time viewing the door, and had recounted to me the way in which the prisoner was guarded. I would willingly give you the description, but this recollection is too distressing.

> Is there a need that I recount
> A keeping guard of unequalled care,
> Walled-up room, narrow space,
> Some little bit of air the only mercy;
> > Days without sun,
> > Nights without sleep,
> Three doors in six feet of space?
> To paint for you such an apartment,
> Would bring forth your tears;
> I have done it by degrees,
> This lamentation has some charms for me.

If night hadn't come, they could never have pulled me away from that place. It was finally necessary to return to the inn, and the next day we turned aside from the Loire, leaving it at our right hand. I was very displeased, not that rivers have been lacking in our journey.

> From that place as far as the Limousin
> We have passed four of them on the way,
> At the very least: at least I recall
> The Indre, the Cher, the Creuse, and the Vienne.
> > These are not mere streams,

> No, no, the map names them for us;
> Those who have perished beneath their waters,
> Have not been to Rome to say Mass.

The first that we encountered was the Indre [*recte:* Cher]. After having passed it, we found on its bank three men of rather good countenance, but badly dressed and very shabby. One of these Guzmanesque heroes[7] had braided his hair, which hung down behind him like a horse's tail. Not far from there we caught sight of some Phyllises [gypsies], I mean Phyllis of Egypt, who approached us dancing, frolicking, displaying their shoulders, and leading after them some duennas, likewise detestable, and who looked at us with as much contempt as if they had been beautiful and young. I shuddered in horror at this spectacle, and couldn't eat for more than two days. Two very fair-complexioned women walked afterward: they were of delicate hue, well shaped, of average beauty, and, to speak rightly, were but angels while the others were real demons. We saluted these two with much respect, as much because of them as for their skirts, which truly were richer than such a suite of persons seemed to promise. The rest of their dress consisted of a cape of white material, and on their heads a little hat *à l'anglaise,* of colored taffeta with silver ribbon. They returned our greeting only by a slight inclination of the head, always walking with the gravity of goddesses, and almost not deigning to cast their eyes on us, simple mortals that we were. Some other duennas followed them, no less ugly than the preceding ones, and a Franciscan friar brought up the rear of the caravan. The baggage was carried in a file, partly on wagons, partly on beasts of burden, then came four empty coaches and some servants round about,

> Not without squirrels and *turquets* [a type of small, hairless dog],
> Nor, I think, without parrots.

All were escorted by Monsieur de la Fourcade, an armed guard. I leave it to you to guess what sort of people these were.[8] Since they were following our route and disembarking at the same inn where our coachman had let us off, we all had scruples about sleeping in the same beds with them and drinking from the same glasses. No one tormented herself more about this than the countess.

The following day we went to sleep at Montels [probably Manthelan], and dined the next day at Port-de-Piles, where our group began to separate. The countess sent a servant, not to her husband's place, but to the house of one of her relatives, to bring news of her arrival and to order that a coach be brought to her with an escort of some sort. As for me, since Richelieu was only five leagues away, I had no chance of missing to go see it; the Germans go quite out of their way for that by several days. Monsieur de Châteauneuf, who knew the countryside, offered to accompany me; I took him at his word, and thus your uncle remained alone, and went to sleep at Châtellerault, where we promised to go early the next day.

Port-de-Piles is a place of passage, where one finds all sorts of means of transportation, even inconvenient ones. One meets up with wretched horses,

> Still poorly shod, and worse fitted with bits,
> And very badly harnessed.

But what the deuce! we had no choice! Such as they were, I had them put in condition,

> Leave the worst, and mount the best.[9]

For greater security, we took a guide whom we had to ride behind, one after the other, in order to gain time. With that we only had to do what was necessary in order to see the most remarkable things. I had promised to sacrifice a black ewe to the southern winds, a white one to the Zephyrs, and to Jupiter the fattest ox I could find in the Limousin: all were favorable to us.[10] I believe however that it will suffice that I pay them in songs, for the oxen of the Limousin are too expensive, and there are some that sell for a hundred *écus* in the region.

Having arrived in Richelieu, we began with the château, the description of which I will, however, send to you only on the first day. What I can roughly tell you about the town is that it will soon have the glory of being the most beautiful village in the universe.[11] Little by little it is deserted because of the infertility of the soil, or for being four leagues away from all rivers and all thoroughfares. In that, its founder, who claimed to create a town of renown, did not make proper preparations, something that he did not do very often.

I am astonished, since it is said he could do everything, that he didn't have the Loire transported to the foot of that new town, or that he didn't have the main road to Bordeaux pass by. Failing that, he should have chosen another site, and he indeed had this thought; but the desire to consecrate the traces of his birth obliged him to build around the room where he was born.[12] He had some of those vanities that many people will censure, and which are nevertheless common to all the heroes: witness that one of Alexander the Great, who ordered left behind, wherever he passed, bits and bridles larger than usual, in order that posterity might believe that he and his men were another sort of human beings, since they used such large horses.[13] Perhaps also the old park of Richelieu and the woods with their avenues, which were beautiful, seemed to their master worthy of a château more sumptuous than the one of his patrimony; and that château attracted the town, as the main feature creates an accessory.

> In a word it [the town] is, in my opinion,
> Badly situated and well constructed;
> All of the lodgings have been made
> With an equal symmetry.
>
> There are very tall buildings,
> Their appearance would please you without fault;
> The interiors have some defects,
> The greatest being that they lack inhabitants.
>
> Most are vacant;
> I didn't see anyone in the street.
> It displeased me; I like in the cities
> A little noise and crush of people.
>
> I said the street, and I said rightly,
> For it is the only one, and of the straightest.
> May God give it the possibility,
> Of one day seeing itself with junior branches.[14]
>
> You will recall indeed
> That at each end is a public place,
> Large, square, and of identical shape,
> Which, without doubt, has fine elegance.

> This is also all there is, but it's sufficient:
> To know whether the town is strong,
> I refer to its moats,
> Walls, parapets, ramparts, and gates.

Moreover, I cannot better describe to you all these lodgings of the same adornment than by the Place Royale [des Vosges, in Paris]: the interiors are much more somber, you can well believe, and less furnished.

I forgot to indicate to you who were the financial and cabinet officers, secretaries of state, and other personages attached to that cardinal, who had the majority of these buildings constructed to oblige him and to form a court for him.[15] The fine wits [*beaux esprits*] would have followed their examples, were it not that they are not great builders, as Voiture says;[16] for, in other respects, they were all full of zeal and affection for that great minister. There you have what I had to tell you concerning the town of Richelieu. I am delaying the description of the château for another time in order to have more frequent occasion to ask you about your news, and in order to contrive a diversion that will make you spend our exile with less annoyance.

At Châtellerault, 5 September 1663.

Letter V

I PROMISED YOU BY THE LAST POST THE DESCRIPTION OF THE CHÂTEAU of Richelieu; rather cursorily in order not to tell you untruths, and without taking into consideration my slight memory or the trouble that this enterprise was bound to give me. As for the trouble, I do not speak about it, and devoted husband that I am, I want to examine it well. That which restrains me is my flawed memory, being able to say most of the time that I have seen nothing of what I have seen—to such an extent I well know how to forget things. Despite that, I think it best not to pass over this point in my travels without giving you an account of it. However badly I carry this out, there will always be something of benefit; and it will only be preferable for you to know, if not the entire history of Richelieu, at least some singularities that have not escaped me, because I paid particular attention to them. They are not perhaps the most remarkable, but what does that matter to you? Knowing your turn of mind, a whimsical account of these matters will please you more than so many learned and particular observations. Those who will look for these learned observations in my letters to you will be making a big mistake; you know my ignorance in architectural matters, and what I said about Vaux[-le-Vicomte] was based only on others' reports;[1] the same advantage is not lacking for Richelieu. Truly, instead of that, I have had information from the concierge and from Monsieur de Châteauneuf; with God's help and that of these persons, I will succeed. Don't fail to suppose the worst, for it is better, it seems to me, to be mistaken in this way than in the other. In any case, you will have recourse to what Monsieur Desmarets has said about this house. He is a great master in matters of description; I would well refrain from giving details about any of the places where he has taken the pleasure to stretch his limbs, if it wasn't that the way in which I write to you about these things has nothing in common with that of his *Promenades*.[2]

We arrived then at Richelieu by an avenue which borders one

side of the park. According to the truth, that avenue may be a half league in length, but in reckoning pursuant to the impatience I was in, we found that it was a good league at the very least. Never was a prelude found to be so inappropriate and has seemed so long to me. At length we found ourselves in a very spacious square. I do not quite recall its shape: semicircular or half-oval, that doesn't matter for the story, and provided that you are informed that it is the main entrance of that house, it suffices. Neither do I remember of what the base court, fore court, and subsidiary courts are composed of, nor of the number of pavilions and *corps-de-logis* of the château, still less of their structure.[3] These details have escaped me, and once again you are a woman not to trouble yourself very much about them. It is sufficient that the whole is of a beauty, a magnificence, a grandeur worthy of him who had it built. The moats are broad and filled with very pure water. After passing over the [fixed] drawbridge, you find the gate guarded by two gods, Mars and Hercules.[4] I strongly praised the architect[5] for having placed them at that post, for although Apollo sometimes served as a mere clerk to the secretaries of His Eminence, Mars and Hercules could well serve him as Swiss guards. It would be worth my pausing over them a bit more if that gate did not offer features still more remarkable. You will especially recall that it is covered with a dome, and that there is a figure of Fame at the summit. She is a goddess who doesn't delight in being locked away, and who prefers to be in that location rather than being given as her retreat the most beautiful apartment of the dwelling.

> She is also in a pose
> All prepared to take flight;
> One foot in the air, a trumpet in each hand,
> Light, and unfurling her wings,
> As if going to carry the tidings
> Of the actions of Richelieu,
> Cardinal, duke, and demigod.
> Such, in short, she must be
> In order to well serve such a good master;
> For so much the less has she leisure
> So much the more it gives her pleasure.[6]

This figure is of bronze and very esteemed. At the two sides of the frontispiece that I am describing have been erected, in the fashion of statues, of pyramids if you wish, two columns from the shafts of which emerge prows of ships[7] (prows of ships [*bouts de navires*] will scarcely please you, and perhaps you would prefer the term "points" or "beaks": choose the least bad of these three words. I strongly doubt that even one is correct; but I prefer to use it rather than call them rostral columns). They are the remnants of an amphitheater that was found very much by good luck, there being nothing that better suits the admiralship, which title was added to so many others by the one who had this château constructed.[8] Within the courtyard and on the pediment of the same entrance, one sees three little Hercules, as plump and as pretty as little Hercules can be;[9] each of them is furnished with his lion's skin and club. (Doesn't that make you recall that Saint Michael, provided with his devil?) The sculptor, in giving them the faces of an old man and proportioning them to his stature, has also given them the air of children, which renders the work so pleasant that in case of need they would pass for Pastimes or Laughter, a bit stout limbed, it is true. This entire frontispiece is the composition of Jacques Lemercier, and it has on each side a wall with a terrace that overlooks the whole house, and from which it appears that two pavilions at the two ends communicate with each other.

If the remainder of the dwelling is as arresting to me to the same degree as is the entrance, there will not be a letter here but a volume. What to do about this? It is quite proper that I use the leisure that the king gives us for something. Around the château are a great many busts and statues, most antique, as you could say of the Jupiters, Apollos, Bacchuses, Mercuries, and others of the same worth;[10] for concerning the gods, I know them well, but concerning the heroes and great persons, I am not very expert. I even remember that in looking at these masterpieces, I took Faustina for Venus (to which of the two must I give honorable reparations?). And since we are speaking of Venus, there are four of them by good report in Richelieu, one among them divinely beautiful, and about which Monsieur de Maucroix said that Poussin spoke to him a good deal, even placing it above the *Medici Venus*.[11] Among the other statues which have their rooms and their niches there, Apollo and Bacchus carry the prize according to the taste of the learned.[12] It was however Mercury that I examined more, because of those swallows who are so naïve as to entrust their little ones to him, all thief that he is. Read that passage in the *Promenades de Richelieu;*[13] it seemed beautiful to me, as well as the description of those two captives, of whom Monsieur Desmarets says that one bears his chains patiently, the other with strength and constraint.[14] They have been placed in a notable place, namely, at the site of the great stair, one on one side of the vestibule, the other on the other side;[15] which is a sort of consolation for these marbles, of which Michelangelo could have fashioned two emperors.

> One yet regrets his fate,
> The other seems slightly less mutinous.
> Fortunate captives! If that can be said[16]
> Of a hard marble and of a chained man.
>
> I would not want to be one or the other
> To adorn such a delightful abode;
> In other circumstances your sex and ours
> Prides itself equally on one of the two.
>
> We pride ourselves in being slaves of women,
> You pride yourself in being like marble for us;
> But it is in verse that the chains and passions [of love]
> Are very common and have nothing but gentleness.

Excuse me for this small digression; it is impossible for me to come across that word "slave" without pausing. What can you expect? Everyone loves to talk about his craft; this may be said however without wronging you. To return to our two captives, I certainly think there have been in former times some slaves of your kind that were esteemed, but they would scarcely be the equal of these. They say that it is not possible to see anything more excellent, and that in these statues Michelangelo surpassed not only the modern sculptors, but also many works of the ancients. There is a passage which is as if only roughed-out:[17] either Death, unable to tolerate the completion of a work which was to be immortal, had stopped Michelangelo at that place, or that that great person had done so intentionally, in order that posterity recognized that no one was capable of touching a figure after him. However that may be, I only esteem these two captives the more, and I maintain that the master derives as much glory from what they lack as from what he has given to them that is most finished.

LETTER V

> May there be no complaint that the work has been
>> found imperfect;
> Its worth is greater, its author more lamented,
>> Than if he had finished it.[18]

Instead of ascending to the rooms by the great stair, as we should have, being so close to it, we allowed ourselves to be guided by the concierge; that made us lose the opportunity of seeing it, and no mention of it was made. Monsieur de Châteauneuf himself, who had seen it, didn't remember to speak about it.

> For which I am in no way grateful to him;
> For other people have told me that they had
>> admired
>>> That stair,
> And that it is of veined marble.[19]

For me it is neither the marble nor the jasper that I miss, but the antiquities that are upstairs, particularly that favorite of the emperor Hadrian, Antinoüs, who in his statue contended in beauty and handsome countenance with Apollo, with however this difference, that the latter had the air of a god and the other of a man.

I shall not amuse myself by describing to you the various enrichments nor the furniture of this palace; that which can be said of its beauty, Monsieur Desmarets has said. Then we almost didn't have the leisure to look at these things, the hour and the concierge making us pass from room to room, without us halting before original Albrecht Dürers, Titians, Poussins, Peruginos, Mantegnas, and other heroes,[20] whose kind is as common in Italy as are army generals in Sweden.

There was however a place where I lingered for a long time. I was not minded to notice whether it was a cabinet or an antechamber; however that may be, the room is tapestried with portraits,[21]

> For the most part about as large
> As dressing-table mirrors.
> If we had had more time,
> Less haste, a different guide,
> I would have told you what people.

You may judge that they are not people of small worth. I interested myself especially in Cardinal de Richelieu, a cardinal who will hold more space in history than thirty popes; in the duke [de Richelieu][22] who inherited his name, his virtues, his fine inclinations, and his château; in the late admiral de Brézé.[23] It's a pity that he died so young, for everyone speaks of him as being a seigneur who was marvelously accomplished, and truly to be compared with Mars [Condé?], Armand [Richelieu], and Neptune. Monsieur le Prince [Condé] and he had undertaken to fill the world with their wonders: Monsieur le Prince the earth, and the Duc de Brézé the sea. The first has completed his enterprise, the other would have advanced very far if he had lived, but a cannon shot stopped him, picking him out in the midst of a naval force. I don't know if they showed me the marquis [de Richelieu][24] and the abbé de Richelieu;[25] there is the likelihood however that their portraits are also in that cabinet, although they were only children when it was arranged as it is. Both are very worthy to have places there. As long as the marquis lived, he was loved by the king and the beauties; the abbé is loved by everyone by a fatality whose cause is not to be looked for among the stars.[26]

In addition to the family of Richelieu, I surveyed that of Louis XIII. The remainder is filled with our kings and queens, great lords, great personages of France (I make two classes of great personages and great lords, well knowing that in all things it is good to avoid confusion). In short, this cabinet is the history of our nation. They took good care not to forget the persons who have triumphed over our kings. Don't go and imagine that I mean by that Englishmen or Spaniards; it is a much more formidable and much more powerful people of whom I wish to speak. In one word, they are the Jocondes, the Belle-Agnèses, and those illustrious conquerers, without whom Henri IV would have been an invincible prince.[27] I looked at them with as much pleasure as I would like to see your uncle at a hundred leagues from here.

At last we left that place and traversed I don't know how many rooms, rich, magnificent, adorned as best as can be, and about which I shall say nothing; for to divert myself over paneling and gilding—I whom Richelieu has filled with originals and antiquities—you would not advise me to do so. Nevertheless I will confess to you that the king's apartment seemed to me marvelously superb; that of the queen is no less so. There is so much gold that in the end I was bored. Consider what the great lords can do, and what misery it is to be rich: it was necessary to invent rooms of stucco, where magnificence hides itself under the appearance of simplicity. It is even good that you know that the king's apartment consists of several rooms, one of which, called the Grand Cabinet, is filled with exquisite paintings.[28] There are among others some Bacchanals by Poussin,[29] and a burlesque and enigmatic combat between Pallas and Venus by a painter whom the concierge could not name for us [Perugino, *Combat of Love and Chastity* (Louvre, 1503–5)]:[30] Venus wears a helmet on her head and carries a long sword.[31] I would very much like to remember the other incidents of this combat and the different personages who compose the painting, for each of these goddesses has her partisans. You would find very amusing the visions which the painter has had. He leaves the advantage to the daughter of Jupiter, but by the way, they are both his daughters; I was wanting therefore to speak about the one who was born from his brain. Poor Venus is wounded by her enemy;[32] by which the artist has depicted things not as they are (for it is usually beauty that is victorious over virtue) but rather as they should be; assuredly his mistress had played some bad trick on him.

This Grand Cabinet of which I speak is accompanied by another small one, where four paintings full of little figures represent the Four Elements.[33] These paintings are by [*crossed out:* Rembrant]; the concierge told us so, if I am not mistaken, and if I would be mistaken, they would be no less the Four Elements. One sees there fireworks, tiltings at the ring, carousels, amusements with sleds, and other similar bagatelles.[34] If you ask me what all this means, I shall reply to you that I know nothing about it.

Moreover, the Cardinal de Richelieu, as the cardinal that he was, took care that his château was sufficiently furnished with chapels. There are three, of which we saw the two upstairs; as for the one downstairs, we didn't have time to see it, and I regret this because of a Saint Sebastian that is highly esteemed.[35] In one of those that is upstairs, I found the original of that plump woman which our cousin has placed over the fireplace of his hall. It is a Magdalen by Titian,[36] fat and corpulent and very pleasant, with beautiful breasts, as in the early stages of her penitence, before the fasting had started to gain on her. (These new female penitents are dangerous, and every man of sound judgment will flee them.)

It seems to me that I have not spoken too devoutly about the

Magdalen; also it's not my business to reason about spiritual matters; I have been in a bad state of grace my entire life: that is why I shall silently pass over the rarities of these two chapels, and I shall pause only at a Saint Jerome, all of inlaid work, most of the pieces as large as pinheads, some like mites.[37] There is not one of them that has been used with its color; nevertheless their combination forms a Saint Jerome so finished, that the brush could not have done better: also, it appears as a painting, even to those who look closely at this work. I admired not only the artifice but also the patience of the artisan. However one considers his enterprise, it cannot be other than unique,

>And in the art of *leveling*,[38]
>The creator of this Saint Jerome
>Must have without doubt excelled
>All the people of the kingdom.

It isn't that I know his birthplace, to speak frankly, nor even his name; but it is right to say that he is a Frenchman, in order to make this marvel appear so much the greater. I would like, as the height of trifling,[39] that another person undertake to count the pieces which compose it.

But will I myself not pass as a trifler[40] by pausing so long over this Saint Jerome? I must leave it; for I must reserve my praises for that famous table of which you must have heard people speak, and which constitutes the principal ornament of Richelieu.[41] It has been placed in the Salon, that is to say, at the end of the Gallery, the Salon being separated from it only by an arched opening. It seems to me that I would have done well to invoke the Muses in order to speak about that table with sufficient dignity.

>It is composed of inlaid pieces,
>And each piece is a treasure;
>For they are all precious stones,
>Agates, jasper, and cornelians;
>Stones of value, noble stones,
>Stones of pomp and of renown;
>There now indeed are some gems:
>Consider that in my life
>I haven't found some object that was so precious.
>That which is prized in the carpets of Persia and Turkey,

> Florets, decoration, animals, embellishments,
>> All that presents itself to the eyes.
> The needle and the brush do not succeed better.
>> I admired each of its shapes;
> And who wouldn't admire what is born under heaven?
> The skill of Pallas, aided by dyeing,
> Yields to the happy whims of simple Nature;
>> Chance produces pieces
> That Art has no more to do than join together, and
>> which produce without painting
> Perfect models of florets and of birds.

All of that however counts for nothing: that which constitutes the value of that table is an agate[42] in the center, almost as large as a basin, cut as an oval and of extremely vivid colors. Its veins are delicate and mixed with dead leaf, dun, and dawn color: moreover, a true agate of the Orient, which has all the qualities one can wish in stones of that type,

> And to sum it up, the queen of agates.

Within the entire empire of cameos (they are a population of stones of which agates form a branch), I don't believe that a marvel yet exists as large as this, nor that anything rarer has come down to us

> From the shores where the sun begins his course.

I make exception for that agate that depicts Apollo and the nine Muses;[43] for I place this first and that of Richelieu second.

> That palace, so famous, of the Florentine princes,
> Rich and brilliant abode of magnificence;
> The treasure of San Marco: the one to which the French
> Commend the safe-keeping of the ashes of their kings;
> The vast storehouses with which the Seraglio abounds,
> Storehouses enriched with the spoils of the world;
> Jules [Mazarin], after all, never had anything more precious.

And to express myself familiarly, and in less poetical terms,

Saint-Denis and San Marco, the palace of the Grand-Duke
[Palazzo Pitti, Florence],
The Hôtel de Mazarin, the Seraglio of the Great Turk,
Have nothing more notable according to what is said.
I made inquiries about the price of that table:
Would you like to know it? Put up one hundred thousand *écus*,
Double that, add one hundred more to that,
The sum will be its true value.

In the same location where this was placed are four or five busts and some statues, among which they named for me Tiberius and Livia; these are personages whom you know, and about whom Monsieur de la Calprenède[44] talks to you sometimes. I won't say anything more to you about them, for my letter begins to seem a bit long to me. It is however impossible for me not to speak about a certain bust, the drapery of which is of jasper: fine head, but badly combed; facial features homely, although well proportioned, and which have something heroic and wild all at the same time; a proud and terrible look; in short, the true image of a young Scythian. You would never take this head for that of one of our gallants; but then, it's that of Alexander.[45] I might have wronged this prince if, after him, I had looked at a lesser hero than the great Armand. We returned to the latter in the Gallery. One sees there that minister painted in the costume of a cavalier and cardinal, encouraging the troops by his presence, and mounted upon a perfectly beautiful horse.[46] This could well be that Barbary steed whom they called l'*Impudent,* an animal without regard or respect, and who, before Majesties and Eminences, whinnied at all the mares who pleased him. The paintings in that Gallery represent some of the conquests that we have made under the ministry of Armand.[47]

After I had glanced at the main ones, we went down into the gardens, which are without doubt beautiful and very extensive; nothing separates them from the park. This park is a country; deer is hunted here. As for the gardens, the flowerbed is large and the work of more than a day. To make it it was necessary to slice off the entire top of a mountain. The earth embankments are covered with a palisade of *phillyrea,* apparently old, for they are bare in many places: it is true that the statues placed there make amends in some way for its ruined beauty.[48] These locales, as you know, are usually the neighborhood of Floras. I saw one there as well as a Venus, a modern Bacchus, a Consul (what is that Consul doing there among some young goddesses?), a Greek lady, another Roman woman with another lady emerging from the bath. Admit the truth; that lady coming from the bath is not one that you would least gladly see. I cannot tell you how she is built, having only looked at her very briefly. The end of day and the curiosity to see a part of the gardens were the cause of this. From the place where we were looking at these statues, one sees on the right a very extensive lawn, and then some deep, covered, pleasant avenues, and where I would take extreme delight in having an amorous adventure: in a word, among these enemies of day so celebrated by the poets. At noon, indeed, one catches a glimpse of something there,

> As in the evening when the shadows arrive in a room;
> Or when it is no longer night but not yet day.[49]

I went deep into one of these avenues, Monsieur de Châteauneuf, who was tired, let me go. Scarcely had I taken ten or twelve steps, than I felt myself compelled by a secret force to begin a few verses to the glory of great Armand. I have since finished them from the recollections that the nymphs of Richelieu gave me: in truth I missed their presence too soon; it would be desirable to have completed these verses in the same place which had led me to make their first draft. Imagine that I am in a garden avenue, where I meditate upon what follows:

> Shades of the great Armand, if those who are no more
> May still taste of vain honors,
> Receive this tribute from the least of the Muses.
> Formerly her sisters were confused about your goodness;
> Also they have not seen that with an ungrateful silence
> Phoebus had suppressed the brilliance of your good deeds.
> Her children have sung of the losses of Spain,[50]
> And the inevitable destiny for us to be prosperous,
> Everywhere where your resolutions, more feared than the god Mars,
> Have carried the terror of our proud banners;
> They have depicted the winds and Fortune,
> Vainly indignant about the wrong done to Neptune,
> When you held that god enchained for so long:[51]

The rampart which sheltered a mutinous people,
Our neighbors[52] envious of our crown,
And the kings of the sea,[53] and the sea itself
Could not halt the course of your efforts.
The Seine again saw you triumphant on her shores:
What did the people of Permessus[54] not do then!
They heard sung to you your deeds, your wisdom,
Your heroic projects, your various triumphs;
The sound continues yet to the ends of the universe.
I can only add to it a simple prayer:
May the darkness of any age not restrict the course
Of this fame—so fine, so great, so glorious!
May Flora and the Zephyrs not leave these locales!
May their beauty like your name be lasting!
May their master have a favorable fate according to his wishes!
May he sometimes come to visit this abode,
And always be content with the prince and his court!

    I would still be at the end of this avenue where I began these verses if Monsieur de Châteauneuf had not come to alert me that it was late. We passed through the forecourt again in order to get to the other side of the gardens sooner. When we were near the drawbridge, an old servant approached us very politely, and asked me what I thought of Richelieu. I replied to him that it was a faultless house, but that not being able to see everything, we would return the next day, and that we would acknowledge his courtesies and the offers that he made to us (I forgot about our promise).[55] "They never fail to say that," the man replied, "every day I am tricked by the Germans." Without fearing to offend us, and consequently to receive nothing, he would have added, I think: "So much the more will I be by the French." I also saw clearly that Monsieur de Châteauneuf's breeches seemed a bad omen to him.[56] That made me laugh, and I gave him something.

    Scarcely had we dismissed him than the little daylight there was departed from us. We did not omit to go deeper into other avenues, not at all as dark as the preceding ones; they may be so in two hundred years. In all this corner I only noticed a mall and two open-air tennis courts, one of which indeed may be turned toward the east, and the other toward the south or toward the north; I am certain it is one of the two: these courts are apparently used at different times of the day, in order not to have the sun in one's face. From the place where they are, it was necessary to return through new darkness, and walk for some time without seeing one another, at long last finding ourselves again in that square in front of the château, I very satisfied, and Monsieur de Châteauneuf, who was wearing high boots, very tired.

At Limoges, 12 September 1663.

Letter VI

This journey would be a fine thing if one didn't have to get up so early in the morning.¹ Tired as we were, Monsieur de Châteauneuf and I, he for having made the entire circuit of Richelieu in high boots, which I believe I wrote to you about (not failing to omit such a remarkable detail), I for diverting myself by writing to you instead of sleeping. Our promise and the fear of making the carrier wait obliged us to arise before Aurora was awakened. We prepared to take leave of Richelieu without seeing it. It happened unfortunately for us, and yet more unfortunately for the seneschal, whose sleep we were forced to interrupt, that the gates were found to be closed by his order. There was a rumor that some gentlemen of the province had formed a plot to save certain prisoners, suspected of the murder of the Marquis de Faure.² My usual impatience made me curse that encounter. I only praised with restraint the prudence of the seneschal. In order to satisfy me, Monsieur de Châteauneuf spoke to him, and told him that we were carrying the king's mail. Immediately he gave order to open for us; so that we had time to spare, and arrived at Châtellerault, which they persuaded us was only halfway [to Poitiers or Limoges?]

We found your uncle there at a friend's house. They had promised him horses to complete his journey, and he had resolved to omit Poitiers, as being the longest way, provided that I didn't have too great a curiosity to see that city. I contented myself with his account of it, and his friend begged him not to depart unless he was pressed by the officer who accompanied him. We granted only one day to that friend; it wasn't that he depended on us to grant him more (Monsieur de Châteauneuf being a gentleman and fulfilling such commissions to the wishes of those he guided, as well as the court); but we judged that it was better to punctually obey the orders of the king.

Everything that can be imagined in the way of sincerity, civility, good cheer, and good taste was employed to entertain us. The Vienne river passes at the foot of Châtellerault, and in this region it carries carps which are small when they are only half an ell in length. They served us some of the finest with melons which the master of the house scorned, but which seemed excellent to me. In short, that day passed with a not indifferent pleasure; for we were not only among friends, but among relatives.

I found in Châtellerault a member of the Pidoux family,[3] whose sister-in-law had been married by our host. All of the Pidoux have prominent noses, abundantly so.[4] They assured us moreover that they lived a long time, and that death, which is such a common happenstance among other people, was considered as a prodigious event among those of that lineage. I was extremely curious to know if that was true.[5] However that may be, my relative from Châtellerault[6] stays eleven hours on horseback without inconvenience, although he is more than eighty years old. What is extraordinary about him (unlike his relatives in Château-Thierry) is that he loves hunting and tennis, knows the Bible, and writes books on religious questions: he is moreover the jolliest man you ever saw, and who thinks the least about his concerns, except those concerning his pleasure. I believe he has married more than once; the wife he now has is well built and certainly has some merit: I am thankful to her for one thing, that she cajoles her husband and lives with him as if he were her gallant. And I am thankful to her husband for one thing, that he still gives her children. There is thus happy old age, in which pleasures, love, and the graces keep company until the end; there aren't many such, but there are some, and this is one of them. To tell you what is the family of this relative, and how many children he has, I haven't taken notice of this, my mood in no way being to pause over these little people.

Even better, they showed me an adolescent girl whom I gladly gazed upon, and to whom smallpox has bequeathed some graces and has taken some away. It's a shame, for they say that never a girl has had finer expectations than this one.

> What curses
> Do you not deserve, cruel malady,
> Who can only look with envy upon
> The subject of our passions!
> Without your poison, cause of so many tears,
> My relative would have done me honor by half again as much:

> Yet it is a great happiness
> That she has had such a number of charms;
> You have not destroyed everything; her mouth testifies to this,
> Her eyes, her features, and other beautiful things.
> You left her lilies, however much you took her roses;
> And as she is my distant relative,
> I would have taken very great pleasure,
> You may believe, in telling it to her;
> I had the will to do it, but not the leisure:
> This admission can suffice for her.

They assured us that she danced well, and I had no difficulty believing it. That which pleased me more was the tone of her voice and her eyes; her temperament also seemed gentle to me. Moreover, do not ask me anything personal about her, for to speak frankly I conversed little with her, and about indifferent matters. I was quite resolved, if we had stayed longer at Châtellerault, to turn her over on as many sides until I would have discovered what was in her soul, and if she is capable of a secret passion. I cannot inform you about anything else, except that she likes novels very much; it is for you, who also likes them very much, to judge what consequence can be drawn from this.[7] Aside from this relative in Châtellerault, I must have a first cousin in Poitiers, whom I have no recollection of having been told anything about. I only remember because he once brought me to court.

Poitiers is what is properly called a *villace*,[8] which in houses as well as in plowable land may have a circuit of two or three leagues: a badly paved town, full of students, abundant in priests and monks. In recompense there are a number of beautiful women, and they make love as willingly as in any place on earth; I know this from the countess. I had some regret about not going there; you would easily be able to guess the reason.

> It is neither the Pierre-Levée,
> Nor the rock Passe-Lourdin:[9]
> To tell you my thought,
> I have omitted them without regret;
> And as for that other cousin,
> My soul is entirely cured of her,
> But I would much like to have seen
> La Landru.[10]

> Yet having a tender heart,
> I am certain that Cupid
> Would never have failed to seize me
> If he had set that bait for me;
> And so here I am a fine fellow,
> For upon leaving, I have to kick myself:[11]
> I would be sorry to have seen
> > La Landru.

However, I would have seen her if we had continued on our route; I had already found a means of doing so, which I will relate to you.

To return to Châtellerault, you will know that it is half-Huguenot and half-Catholic, and that we have nothing to do with the former. The appointed time that we had stipulated with our host having elapsed, it was necessary to take leave of him; this wasn't done without him renewing his prayers. We gave him as much time as was possible for us, and gave him good thanks, that is to say by breakfasting well, and staying a long time at table, so that there only remained some time to get to Chauvigny, a miserable resting-place, whence begin the bad roads and the smell of garlic, two features which distinguish the Limousin from the other regions of the world.

Our second night's lodging was Bellac. The approach to that place seemed to me a strange thing, and which is worth the trouble of being described. When of eight or ten persons who have passed it without getting off a horse or out of a coach, there are only three or four whose necks are broken, they thank God.

> There are pieces of rocks
> Piled up one upon the other,
> And which cause coachmen to say
> Terrible paternosters.
>
> In the end, this road
> Exhausts the patience
> Of the wisest.
> Who only murmurs there,
> > Without swearing,
> Gains a hundred years indulgence.

Monsieur de Châteauneuf would have cursed it a hundred times,

If at first I hadn't spoken:
"Let us not complain about our troubles;
This rude and little-beaten path
Is going to be the one that leads
To Virtue's abode."[12]

Your uncle replied that it was necessary therefore that we turn away. "It isn't" he added "that there aren't honest people in Bellac, as well as elsewhere, but some circumstances have given a bad odor to its inhabitants." About this subject he told us that being a member of the royal provincial court, he instituted proceedings against a judicial provost of that locality for having forced a beggar to take the place of a criminal condemned to hang, in return for twenty *pistoles* given to that beggar and some assurance of grace with which they lured him. He allowed himself to be led and hoisted up on the gallows very gaily, like a man who was only thinking about his twenty *pistoles,* the provost telling him all the time that he would not be placed in any difficulty, and that grace was going to arrive. In the end the poor devil realized his foolishness, but he only realized it while dropping to his death, a time not at all proper for repenting and making confession. It's a good trick, as you see, and Bellac can boast of having had a provost as bold and as hangable as can be found.[13]

As much as the approaches to that town are vexatious, so is it unpleasant: its mean streets, its badly accommodated and badly proportioned houses. Excuse me, you who are refined, from telling you something about it. In that region they place the kitchen on the *premier étage;*[14] he who has once seen these kitchens hasn't great interest in the sauces that are prepared there. They are people capable of turning a very good morsel into a very bad dish. Although we had chosen the best inn, we drank some "wine" used for dyeing tablecloths, and which is commonly called the "fraud of Bellac." This saying has this good feature, in that Louis XIII is its author.[15]

Nothing would have pleased me without the girl of the house, a young and rather pretty person. I flattered her about her coiffure: it was a type of cap with flaps, of the cutest sort, and bordered by a gold braid three fingers wide. The poor girl, thinking to do the right thing, went immediately to fetch her ceremonial cap to show me. After Chauvigny people almost no longer speak French,[16] but that person understood me without much difficulty; gallant speech is understood in all lands, and has this convenience in that it carries with it its interpreter. However sorry our quarters were, I did not fail to spend a very pleasant night there; my sleep was in no way chequered with dreams, as it usually is. If however Morpheus had led the host's daughter to me, I certainly think I would not have turned her away: he didn't do so and I did without her.

Monsieur Jannart arose before daylight, but his dispatch served for nought, because all our horses being unshod, we had to wait, and for my sins, I revisited the streets of Bellac once more. While I was hurrying the farrier, Monsieur de Châteauneuf, who had undertaken to guide us that day, made inquiries about so many roads, that that served in no little way to make him take the longest and the worst. By chance our journey wasn't great: Since Limoges is only distant from Bellac by a brief day, we had all the leisure time to lose our way, of which we acquitted ourselves very well, and as people who knew neither the language nor the land.

As soon as we arrived, my faithful Achates[17] (who could this be but Monsieur de Châteauneuf?) arranged things for his return, and chose the route of the courier who was to leave the next day. I was displeased that he was leaving us so soon, for in truth, he is a gentleman, and knows how to report court news very gracefully; besides, it seems to me that he doesn't harm his person in the telling. Henceforth we will try to do without him, with even less trouble than remains to inform you about our place of retreat: that deserves an entire letter.[18]

In the meantime, if you desire to know how I am feeling, I shall say to you quite well; and your uncle must be feeling even better, given the testimonies of esteem and goodwill which everyone confers on him. The bishop[19] principally: he is a prelate who has all the fine qualities that you can imagine; magnificent, especially, and who keeps the best table in the Limousin. He lives as a great lord and is one in reality. Don't go and imagine that the rest of the diocese is miserable and disgraced by Heaven, as one imagines in our provinces. I submit to you that the people of Limoges are as proud and as polite as any people in France: the men have some intelligence in this region, and the women some purity, but their costumes,[20] way of living, occupations, compliments especially do not please me; it's a shame that . . . has never married; as for my opinion,

It isn't a pleasant abode.
I find there concerning love's mysteries
Few wise men, many profane ones,
Few Phyllises, many Jeannes,
Little muscat of Saint-Mesmin,[21]
Much drink that is not very healthful,
A lot of garlic and little jasmine:
Judge whether I have any business there.[22]

                At Limoges, 19 September 1663.

Notes

Letter I

1. "Vous ne jouez" can also mean "you do not play" (a musical instrument) or "you do not gamble," but the latter is highly unlikely because gambling ca. 1663 was confined to court circles (to which the La Fontaines did not belong), and because their modest economic status would not have encouraged that activity.
2. See below, Letter VI n7.
3. Cf. Molière, *Les Femmes Savantes* (1672; lines spoken by Clitandre, a young male lover):

> Et les femmes docteurs ne sont point de mon goût.
> Je consens qu'une femme ait des clartés de tout;
> Mais je ne lui veux point la passion choquante
> De se rendre savante afin d'être savante;
> (1.3.217–20)

4. On Jannart and the reasons for his exile to Limoges, see the Introduction.
5. A lieutenant of the provost of Paris who was both police officer and judge.
6. Jannart lived in Paris on the Ile de la Cité, on the Quai des Orfèvres, within the precinct of the Palais, which housed the Parlement. La Fontaine, when in Paris during these years, regularly stayed in his house, which he refers to as "our house" in the next sentence.
7. Their son, Charles de La Fontaine (b. 1653), ten years old in 1663.

Letter II

1. Madame Jannart, aunt to La Fontaine's wife, with whom she shared the same name (Marie Héricart).
2. "The allusion is a wry comment on a passage in Voiture's famous *Chanson sur l'air du branle du Metz,* another *relation [de voyage],* this time of a journey following La Fontaine's itinerary as far as Orléans:

> Nous vîmes dedans la nue
> La tour de Mont-le-héris
> Qui pour regarder Paris
> Allongeait son col de grue.

As with Chapelle, the joke is for the initiated; but La Fontaine's touch is lighter, the triple repetition cleverly underlining the point made by the feigned hesitation" (quoted from David Shaw, "La Fontaine's Letters to his Wife," *Modern Languages* 53 [1972]: 130–31). Vincent Voiture is cited by name at the end of Letter IV; he was an important influence upon La Fontaine, who called himself his disciple as late as 1687 (ibid., 126).

3. An error; the surviving fortress was built in the early thirteenth century under Philip Augustus and modified in the late fourteenth century. See André Châtelain, *Châteaux forts et féodalité en Ile-de-France du XIième au XIIIième siècle* (Nonette: Créer, 1983), 305–10; Jean-Marie Pérouse de Montclos, ed., *Le guide du patrimoine. Ile-de-France* (Paris: Hachette, 1992), 454–56.

4. The walls of these rooms and their (English?) frescoes, visible in La Fontaine's time, are no longer extant, although the outlines of the rooms remain (see Châtelain, *Châteaux forts,* 307 [plan], 308–9 [aerial photo]).

5. La Fontaine (or his first editor in 1729) wrote "Condé," an error for Candé (Brodeau de Candé, *grand maître des eaux et forêts*).

6. La Fontaine's memory is faulty here: Plessis-Pâté precedes Châtres (Arpajon since 1720) on his itinerary.

7. For a number of years the valley was indeed a place where travelers were attacked; the culprits were servants of a local maréchale. See Léon Risch, "Avec La Fontaine sur la route d'Orléans," *Revue de l'histoire de Versailles et de Seine-et-Oise* 39 (1937): 101.

8. A reference to La Fontaine's farm of La Tueterie (now La Fontaine-Regnard or du Regnard), 2 km south of Château-Thierry (Aisne), La Fontaine's place of birth.

9. Cf. the opening lines of La Fontaine's fable, "Le Coche et la Mouche" (*Fables,* bk. 7, fable 9, lines 1–5) :

> Dans un chemin montant, sabolonneux, malaisé,
> Et de tous les côtés au soleil exposé,
>   Six forts chevaux tiraient un coche,
> Femmes, moine, vieillards, tout était descendu;
> L'attelage suait, soufflait, était rendu.

And the singing lady (line 21) is reminiscent of the singing notary in La Fontaine's traveling group.

10. Themis, goddess of justice, who here personifies the king's orders.

11. Cf. "Les Deux Pigeons" (*Fables,* bk. 9, fable 2; in line 20 the phrase "le désir de voir" reappears).

12. A reference to an incident of the Fronde (1652): A rebel army, led by Jacques de Saulx, comte de Tavannes, seized the outskirts of Étampes, where it was engaged by the royal forces led by Turenne. The *frondeurs* burnt down the *faubourgs* and took refuge within the town, where they destroyed all the buildings close to the walls. This was the devastation seen by La Fontaine. Because of the failure of Charles IV of Lorraine, the rebels' ally, to arrive, a treaty was signed which ended the siege on the condition that Charles depart from French soil. This was accomplished.

La Fontaine's depiction of Tavannes blowing on a peashooter is his poetic way of comparing the rebellious count and his forces to mischievous schoolboys.

On the siege of Étampes, see Basile Fleureau, *Les antiquitez de la ville et du duché d'Estampes* (Paris: J. B. Coignard, 1683), part 1, chap. 44, 267–83 (reprint Marseille, 1977).

13. Pierre du Moulin (1568–1658), Protestant theologian.

14. The youngest of the Fates.

15. A monument to Joan of Arc was erected on a pile of this bridge (le Pont des Tourelles), probably in 1458. Composed of a group of bronze figures, it depicted Joan and Charles VII kneeling opposite each other, hands raised in prayer, in front of Christ on the cross and the Virgin (probably standing). This group was mutilated in 1562 or 1567 during the Wars of Religion and rebuilt in 1571, with the dead Christ now on the Virgin's lap at the base of the cross. It was this restoration which La Fontaine saw, although he makes no mention of the Pietà group. A depiction of the restored group is found on the title page (engraved by Léonard Gaultier) of Jean Hordal, *Heroinae nobilissimae Ioannae Darc Lotharingae vvlgo avrelianensis pvellae historia* . . . (Pont-à-Mousson: Apud Melchiorem Bernardum, 1612). Both Joan and the king appear in full armor.

In the eighteenth century the bridge was replaced by the present Pont Georges V; the monument was reerected in the town, but destroyed in 1792 during the Revolution.

The date of the original monument is in dispute, some scholars assigning it to 1502–9; see A. Collin, "Le pont des Tourelles à Orléans (1120–1760). Étude sur les ponts au moyen âge," *Mémoires de la Société archéologique et historique de l'Orléanais* 26 (1895): chaps. XXII and XXIV; E. Jarry, "L'érection du monument de Jeanne d'Arc sur le pont d'Orléans," *Mémoires de la Sociéte archéologique et historique de l'Orléanais* 42 (1911): 501–13. Modern reconstructions of the two monuments are published in the Atlas to vol. 26 of the *Mémoires,* pl. I, figs. 13, 14; repr. in Jacques Debal, *Orléans: une ville, une histoire* (Orléans: X-Nova, 1998), 1:134, 183.

16. A character in *Amadis de Gaula,* a Spanish chivalric romance (1508), translated into French in 1540–48.

17. A reference to the poem *La Pucelle* by Jean Chapelain, partially published in 1656.

Letter III

1. The reference is to hired servants. Caudal provides the following note about those from Sologne (Ange-Marie Caudal, ed., *Lettres de La Fontaine à sa femme ou Relation d'un voyage de Paris en Limousin* [Paris: Centre de documentation universitaire, 1966], 97–98n7):

"On appelle proverbialement un niais de Sologne, celuy qui se trompe à son profit, ces matois qui font les Niais, qui entendent bien

leur compte et qui souvent trompent les autres. Allusion aux proverbes suivants:
> 'Les Solognots sots à demi
> Qui se trompent à leur profit.'
>
> 'Un fol de Soulogne qui s'abuse à son profit.'
>
> 'Quel niais de Sologne! tu te trompes à ton profit.'"

> (from Antoine-Jean-Victor Leroux de Lincy, *Le livre des proverbes français* [Paris: Delahaye, 1859], 1:397)

2. The fourteenth-century church of Notre-Dame de Cléry, built with the support of Philip IV the Fair (r. 1285–1314), was severely damaged by the English in 1428 near the end of the Hundred Years War; it was afterward rebuilt by Charles VII and Jean, Count of Dunois (the Bastard of Orléans). In 1467 Louis XI elevated Cléry to the status of a royal chapel and decided to be buried there rather than at Saint-Denis, the traditional necropolis of French kings. In 1482 Louis inaugurated the addition of the four western bays of the nave.

The tomb of Louis XI (r. 1461–83) was the work of the sculptor Colin d'Amiens, aided by Conrard de Cologne, a goldsmith from Tours, and Laurent Wrine, a metal caster. The king was depicted kneeling in prayer. The tomb was destroyed by the Huguenots in 1562, but restored in 1622 upon order of Louis XIII; it was then that a white marble statue of the king by Michel Bourdin was substituted for the original effigy in gilded bronze. This was the monument seen by La Fontaine. Damaged in the Revolution, the tomb was restored once again in 1894, and is still *in situ* in Notre-Dame de Cléry.

This was an early, important example of the "activated effigy" in French funerary sculpture, a tradition which began in the fourteenth century but became common only in the sixteenth; see Émile Mâle, *L'art religieux de la fin du moyen-âge en France,* 5th ed. (Paris: Armand Colin, 1949), 429–31; Henri Zerner, *L'art de la renaissance en France. L'invention du classicisme* (Paris: Flammarion, 2002), 373–74.

On the preparatory material for this tomb, which goes back to 1474 and involved the sculptor Michel Colombe and the painter Jean Fouquet, see Louis Jarry, *Histoire de Cléry et de l'église collégiale et chapelle royale de Notre-Dame de Cléry* (Orléans: Herluison, 1899), 167–71 and pl. VI (opp. 144); Pierre Pradel, *Michel Colombe, le dernier imagier gothique* (Paris: Plon, 1953), 20; Theodor Müller, *Sculpture in the Netherlands, Germany, France, and Spain 1400 to 1500* (Baltimore: Penguin Books, 1966), 139.

3. Allusion to Charles the Bold, Duke of Burgundy (1433–77) who, in 1468, held Louis XI a virtual prisoner at Péronne and forced him to use his army in league with the Burgundians to attack Liège. La Fontaine probably knew this episode from reading Commynes; see *The Memoirs of Philippe de Commynes,* ed. Samuel Kinser, trans. Isabelle Cazeaux (Columbia: University of South Carolina Press, 1969), 1:bk. II. Commynes at one point described the French king as "terri-

fied" while at Péronne (172). See also Richard Vaughan, *Charles the Bold: The Last Valois Duke of Burgundy* (London: Longman, 1973), 30ff.

4. This sentence was inadvertently omitted by Caudal, ed., *Lettres de La Fontaine,* but Caudal provided a note for it on 100n24. Louis-Tristan l'Hermite was *prévôt des maréchaux de France* since 1451 under Charles VII and Louis XI. He regularly carried out the harsh policies of the latter monarch, and was famous for his contempt for judicial procedures and his cruelty. La Fontaine's mention of him here is a sarcastic reference, redounding upon Louis XI.

5. The following anecdote was directly borrowed by La Fontaine from Théodore Agrippa d'Aubigné, *Les avantures du baron de Faeneste,* bk. 3, chap. 13 (first published in 1630). La Fontaine slightly changed the names of the disputants (Pautrot to Potrot, la dame de Noaillé to Nouaillé). The dialogue between the two, which La Fontaine followed closely in abbreviated form, is given in Henri Régnier, ed., *Oeuvres de J. de La Fontaine,* new ed., (Paris: Librairie Hachette, 1892), 9:240n1.

6. Saint-Solenne was badly damaged by a storm in 1678 and replaced by the present cathedral of Saint-Louis between 1679–1702. However, the apse and west façade, with the upper part of its bell tower in Renaissance style (begun 1544), survived.

7. La Fontaine's fable about the formation of the Beauce region follows in the tradition of Rabelais, who recounted how the Beauce received its name, its fallow land, and the yawning habit of its inhabitants (*Gargantua et Pantagruel,* bk. 1, chap. 16).

8. Gaston d'Orléans.

9. The theme of man's discontent with his condition reappears in the fable "Les Grenouilles qui demandent un roi" (*Fables,* bk. 3, fable 4), as noted by Louis Arnould, *La terre de France chez La Fontaine: bêtes et gens,* 7th ed. (Tours: Alfred Mame et fils, 1932), 29.

10. The château of Blois was built mainly in three stages, in entirely different architectural styles: the Aile Louis XII (1498–1515), the Aile François I (1515–24), and the Aile de Gaston d'Orléans (1635–38), the last designed by François Mansart. See Jean-Marie Pérouse de Montclos, ed., *Le guide du patrimoine. Architectures en région centre: Val de Loire, Beauce, Sologne, Berry, Touraine* (Paris: Hachette, 1988), 159–70.

11. On Gaston's last years at Blois (1653–60), marked by his newfound religiosity and good deeds, see Georges Dethan, *La vie de Gaston d'Orléans* (Paris: Éditions de Fallois, 1992), chap. 10. Dethan (331) believes that La Fontaine's praise of Gaston was an accurate reflection of how his subjects regarded his paternal rule in the Blésois.

12. On this garden, see ibid., 319. Plants from this garden were painted on vellum by Nicolas Robert; see *Collections de Louis XIV. Dessins, albums, manuscrits* (Paris: Éditions des musées nationaux, 1977), 302–11.

13. François de Maucroix (1619–1708) was La Fontaine's closest lifelong friend and part of the circle around Foucquet, who sent him to Italy in 1661 to look for works of art (see below, Letter V n11). On Maucroix, see Philip A. Wadsworth, *Young La Fontaine: A Study of his Artistic Growth in his Early Poetry and First Fables* (Evanston, IL: Northwestern University Press, 1952), 13–14 and pas-

sim. Caudal speculates that his disdain for "bald mountains" (*montagnes pelées*) must have been privately communicated to La Fontaine (*Lettres de La Fontaine*, 107n66).

Letter IV

1. The château of Amboise was built from 1491 to 1498 by Charles VIII; the Aile Louis XII–François I dates from after 1498. See Pérouse de Montclos, ed., *Le guide du patrimoine. Architectures en région centre,* 105–11.

2. The antlers and bones were also remarked upon at length by the scientist and architect Claude Perrault, who visited Blois in 1669; see his *Voyage à Bordeaux (1669)* ed. Paul Bonnefon (Paris: Renouard, 1909), 145. Régnier added (*Oeuvres de J. de La Fontaine,* 9:248n2): "On avait cru longtemps que ce bois de cerf était naturel; mais on reconnut à la fin qu'il était de main d'homme, aussi bien qu'un os du cou et quelques côtes qu'on montrait également."

3. The Tour Hurtault (south) and the Tour des Minimes (north), which contain spiral ramps for the passage of horses. The towers are made of stone; La Fontaine perhaps mistook them for earthenwork because of their coloration, seen in the bad weather of which he speaks.

4. . . . quae quantum vertice ad auras
aetherias, tantum radice in Tartara tendit.
(*Georgics* 2.291–92)

La Fontaine wrote: "D'un bout au ciel, d'autre aux enfers."
Cf. also his fable "Le Chêne et le Roseau" (bk. 1, fable 22, lines 31–32):

Celui de qui la tête au ciel était voisine,
Et dont les pieds touchaient à l'empire des morts.

5. Charles VIII (1470–98) was born in the old château of Amboise, and died there in his new Logis du Roi. Claude de France (1499–1524), the first queen of François I, gave birth to three of seven royal children there: Louise (1515–17), Charlotte (1516–24), and François (1518–36).

6. Nicolas Foucquet, superintendent of finances and builder of the sumptuous château and garden of Vaux-le-Vicomte before his arrest in 1661, was the patron of La Fontaine (see Introduction).

Foucquet was imprisoned briefly at Amboise, from 4–25 December 1661, before being transferred to Vincennes. In 1662 La Fontaine published an anonymous pamphlet, *Élégie aux nymphes de Vaux,* which contains verses appealing to the nymphs of Vaux to influence Louis XIV to be merciful toward Foucquet. See Régnier, ed., *Oeuvres de J. de La Fontaine,* 8:355–58 ("Élégie I: Pour M. Foucquet"); see also Wadsworth, *Young La Fontaine,* 110, and Marie-Hélène Tesnière and Prosser Gifford, eds., *Creating French Culture: Treasures from the Bibliothèque nationale de France* (New Haven, CT: Yale University Press, 1995), 235–36, no. 99.

Also in 1662, La Fontaine wrote an *Ode au Roi* in favor of Foucquet, which he sent to the prisoner (Régnier, ed., *Oeuvres de J. de La Fontaine,* 8:390–93); it was not published until 1671. Foucquet criticized the poem, and La Fontaine's letter of response (30 Jan. 1663) is preserved (ibid., 9:354–56). A few lines from *Le songe de Vaux* (fragment of 1671) also reveal La Fontaine's sympathies toward Foucquet (Titcomb, ed. [as in Letter V n1], 91 [see below]).

7. Similar to Guzmán de Alfarache, the hero of Mateo Alemán's *Vida del Picaro Guzmán de Alfarache* (1599, 1604). It was freely translated into French by Jean Chapelain in 1635. The adjective "Guzmanesque" was invented by La Fontaine.

8. Caudal (*Lettres de La Fontaine*, 116n48) speculates that these women were prostitutes and others (perhaps witches, thieves, and fortune-tellers) being led into exile in the colonies; La Fontaine notes that they were accompanied by an armed guard.

Régnier commented on this (*Oeuvres de J. de La Fontaine*, 9:251–52n6) : "Il y a des édits de 1560, de 1666, etc., qui ordonnent d'attacher les bohémiens ou égyptiens à la chaine, et de les conduire aux galères sans autre forme ni figure de procès, et de fouetter, flétrir, et bannir hors du Royaume les femmes et les filles qui les accompagnent, 'sorcières, larronnesses, et diseuses de bonne aventure.'"

9. A quotation from Clément Marot's "Epistre XVIII: Au Roy" (1531), line 33: "Laisse le pire, & sur le meilleur monte" (*Oeuvres poétiques complètes* [Paris: Bordas, 1990], 1:321).

10. The passage recalls the fable "Jupiter et le Passager" (*Fables*, bk. 9, fable 13, esp. lines 10–17), as noted by Régnier, ed., *Oeuvres de J. de La Fontaine*, 9:254n2.

11. On the town of Richelieu, see esp. Maurice Dumolin, "La construction de la ville de Richelieu," *Bulletin de la Société des antiquaires de l'Ouest* ser. 3, 10 (1934/35): 520ff.; Heinfried Wischermann, "Ein unveröffentlichter Plan der Stadt Richelieu von 1633," *Zeitschrift für Kunstgeschichte* 35 (1972): 302–6; Hanno-Walter Kruft, *Städte in Utopia. Die Idealstadt vom 15. bis zum 18. Jahrhundert. Zwischen Staatsutopie und Wirklichkeit* (Munich: C. H. Beck, 1989), 82–98; Alexandre Gady, *Jacques Lemercier, architecte et ingénieur du Roi* (Paris: Éditions de la Maison des sciences de l'homme, 2005), 278–84 and passim.

12. Richelieu was born on 9 September 1585, but perhaps not at Richelieu; he was baptized in Paris on 5 May 1586 in Saint-Eustache. Mlle. de Montpensier, who visited the château in 1637, wrote that "le Cardinal avoit voulu que l'on conservât la chambre où il étoit né" (*Mémoires de Mlle de Montpensier, petite-fille de Henri IV*, ed. Adolphe Chéruel [Paris: Charpentier, 1858], 1:25). Jean Marot in one of his engravings of the château specified the "Chambre de l'ancien bastiment dans laquelle nâquit le grand Cardinal de Richelieu" (*Le magnifique chasteau de Richelieu . . .* , [Paris? ca. 1650], M16. This and all subsequent references to the plates in this publication follow the numbering in André Mauban, *Jean Marot, architecte et graveur parisien* [Paris: Les Éditions d'art et d'histoire, 1944], 120–21). This "birth-chamber" was located on the left side of the main *corps-de-logis* and formed part of the cardinal's apartment; the room originally was part of the house built by Richelieu's father in 1580, which was incorporated into the new château; see Hilliard Todd Goldfarb, ed., *Richelieu: Art and Power*, exhib. cat. (Montreal: Montreal Museum of Fine Arts, 2002), 254.

13. Plutarch, *Life of Alexander the Great*, 62.

14. The plan of 1634 by Nicolas Tassin shows a number of cross streets, which

still exist (Wischermann, "Ein unveröffentlicher Plan," 302, fig. 1). Perhaps they had not been paved by 1663.

15. For listings of the original house owners, see Dumolin, "La construction de la ville de Richelieu," 551; Wischermann, "Ein unveröffentlichter Plan," 305–6n19. Some of the owners appear listed on the important plan drawn up by Jean Barbet in 1633 (repr. in color in Goldfarb, ed., *Richelieu: Art and Power,* 289, no. 124).

16. Vincent Voiture, in a letter to Pierre Costar, wrote: "Nous autres beaux esprits, nous ne sommes pas grands edificateurs, et nous fondons sur ces vers d'Horace:

> aedificare casas, plostello adjungere mures,
> . . . Si quem delectet barbatum, amentia verset.
> [*Satires,* 2.3.247/249]

(Building toy-houses, harnessing mice to a wee cart, . . .
if these things delighted a bearded man, lunacy would plague him.
Trans. H. Rushton Fairclough, Loeb Classical Library)

Au moins M. de Gombaut, M. de l'Estoile, et moi, avons résolu de ne point bâtir que quand le temps reviendra que les pierres se mettent d'elles-mêmes les unes sur les autres au son de la lyre. Je ne sais si c'est qu'Apollon se soit dégoûté de ce métier-là, depuis qu'il fut mal payé des murailles de Troie; mais il me semble que ses favoris ne s'y adonnent point, et que leur génie les porte à d'autres choses qu'à faire de grands bâtiments" (*Les oeuvres de monsieur de Voiture,* 5th ed. [Paris: Augustin Courbé, 1656], 273 [Lettre CXXV], as quoted in Régnier, ed., *Oeuvres de J. de La Fontaine,* 9:257n1).

Letter V

1. An allusion to the author's *Le songe de Vaux,* still in ms. in 1663. La Fontaine's sources may have included the pages from Madeleine de Scudéry's novel *Clélie, histoire romaine* (Paris and Amsterdam: A. Courbé and J. Blaeu, 1661), 5, pt. 3:1099–142 and the two printed letters on Vaux attributed to André Félibien (n.p., n.d., ca. 1660–61; the only extant copies are in Paris, Bibliothèque Nationale de France, 4°Lk⁷ 10117).

See the following modern edition: Jean de La Fontaine, *Le songe de Vaux,* ed. Eleanor Titcomb (Geneva: Droz, 1967). Written 1659–61, the *Songe* was left unfinished; it was published in fragments beginning in 1665. For its publishing history, see the Titcomb edition, 47–48. See also Tesnière and Gifford, eds., *Creating French Culture,* 235–36, no. 99.

2. Jean Desmarets de Saint-Sorlin, *Les promenades de Richelieu, ou les vertus chrestiennes* (Paris: Henry Le Gras, 1653). Saint-Sorlin (1595–1676), a prolific writer, served as *intendant* of the Duc de Richelieu, the cardinal's nephew and inheritor of the estate. La Fontaine rightly noted that his own style has nothing in common with that of Desmarets. Indeed, the *Promenades,* written entirely in verse, is a combination of description and mysticism: seven of the eight "prome-

nades" are each a sermon consecrated to a different Christian virtue. Despite this, the work contains some interesting descriptive passages, which will be quoted below. It is apparent that La Fontaine carried a copy of the *Promenades* with him on his travels.

3. On the château of Richelieu, see Heinfried Wischermann, *Schloss Richelieu. Studien zu Baugeschichte und Ausstattung,* publ. diss., (University of Freiburg, 1971); Goldfarb, ed., *Richelieu: Art and Power,* 253–55, 287–88, nos. 122, 123; Gady, *Jacques Lemercier,* 264–77 and passim.

The half-oval entrance plaza and subsidiary courtyards leading to the château are clearly shown in Jean Marot's bird's-eye view engraving (Goldfarb, ed., *Richelieu: Art and Power,* 288, no. 123).

4. An engraving by Gabriel Perelle shows the château in detail, with the fixed drawbridge leading to the domed entrance gateway; see Jean-Claude Aubineau, *Richelieu. "Par ordre du Cardinal..."* (Richelieu: J.-C. Aubineau, 1980), 29. The statues of Mars and Hercules were placed in niches flanking the entrance portal. La Fontaine makes no mention of the marble statue of Louis XIII, which stood above the entrance portal. All of the statuary was by Guillaume Berthelot (see the engraving by Marot of the entrance pavilion in Goldfarb, ed., *Richelieu: Art and Power,* 254, fig. 6). The torso and head of the Louis XIII statue survive (Musée des Beaux-Arts, Poitiers; see ibid., 76–77, no. 4).

5. Jacques Lemercier (ca. 1582–1654); he is mentioned by name later in this Letter.

6. The figure of Fame, by Berthelot, is shown in Marot's engraving of the entrance pavilion (as in n4). It had been described in verse earlier by Desmarets de Saint-Sorlin:

> Sur la pointe d'un dome icy semble emplumée
> Partir pour un grand vol la prompte Renommée.
> Autour d'elle je voy ces oyseaux voleter,
> Pour partir avec elle, ou pour la consulter,
> Voulant porter bien-tost sur leurs ailes legeres
> Les discords des François aux terres Estrangeres.
> (*Les promenades de Richelieu,* IVe Promenade, 22)

The last line is an allusion to the Fronde.

7. Visible in the engraving by Marot (as in n4); they survive in the Musée de la Marine, Paris (see following note).

8. Richelieu was appointed *Grand-Maître, Chef et Surintendant de la Navigation et Commerce de France* by Louis XIII in 1626. His Chambre within the château was decorated with painted panels of maritime trophies; Benjamin Vignier, *Le chasteau de Richelieu, ou l'Histoire des dieux et des héros de l'antiquité, avec des réflexions morales,* 2nd ed. (Saumur: Henry Desbordes, 1681), 95 (1st ed. Saumur, 1676). A row of sculpted stone ships' prows with maritime attributes set within panels decorated the Palais-Cardinal, Paris (extant in the Galerie des Proues in the present Palais-Royal).

9. These occupied a niche in the entrance pavilion facing the courtyard (shown in Marot, *Le magnifique chasteau de Richelieu,* M14). Vignier described them as "trois petits Hercules de Marbre antique & tres-beaux" (*Le chasteau de Richelieu,*10); they are depicted in a drawing in the Canini album by Giovanni

Angelo Canini (1632/33); see Marie Montembault and John Schloder, *L'album Canini du Louvre et la collection d'antiques de Richelieu* (Paris: Éditions de la RMN, 1988), 63, 264–65, fig. 62.

10. A list of these is given in Vignier, *Le chasteau de Richelieu,* 13–55. On the sculptures at Richelieu, see Montembault and Schloder, *L'album Canini,* Antoine Schnapper, *Curieux du grand siècle. Collections et collectionneurs dans la France du XVIIe siècle. II- Oeuvres d'art* (Paris: Flammarion, 1994), 138–41, and Domingo Gasparro, "Les sculptures antiques de Richelieu et les dessins perdus de l'album Canini," *Revue du Louvre* 53, no. 1 (2003): 59–66.

11. The *Richelieu Venus,* an antique torso discovered at Pozzuoli and acquired by the cardinal probably shortly before his death in 1642 (see Schnapper, *Curieux du grand siècle,* 139–40). Poussin apparently had seen this work before its shipment to France and reported his high opinion of it to François de Maucroix, when the latter was in Rome in 1661 looking for works of art for Foucquet (ibid., 218). The torso is lost.

The fame of this work was great. In 1665, Paul Fréart de Chantelou reported the following conversation with Gianlorenzo Bernini, to whom he was assigned as guide during the Italian artist's sojourn in France: "We went to Versailles. On the way we talked about statues, painting, and sculpture. I told the Cavaliere that we had one figure in France of great beauty, a *Venus,* which was at Richelieu. Only the torso is antique. He told me at once that he had seen it when it had been discovered at Pozzuoli. Then it was sent to France. It was much more beautiful than the *Medici Venus*" (Paul Fréart de Chantelou, *Diary of the Cavaliere Bernini's Visit to France,* ed. Anthony Blunt, trans. Margery Corbett [Princeton, NJ: Princeton University Press, 1985], 192 [13 September 1665]).

12. Vignier cited five statues of Apollo (*Le chasteau de Richelieu,* 12, 24, 25, 42, 55) and five of Bacchus (21, 29, 37, 43, 46). Statues of both gods were recorded by Canini and some are in museum and private collections (Montembault and Schloder, *L'album Canini,* Apollo: 175–76, no. 13, figs. 64, 64A; 177, no. 15, figs. 69, 69A^1, 69A^2; 177–78, no. 16, figs. 70, 70A; 195–96, no. 55, fig. 149; Bacchus: 178–79, no. 17, figs. 77, 77A; 196, no. 56, fig. 150; 197–98, no. 58, fig. 152).

13. Mainte hirondelle passe avec son aile aiguë,
Consulte de ces Dieux la response ambiguë,
Va cent fois & revient, gazoüillant allentour
De Iupiter, de Mars, de Venus et d'Amour.
Mais n'en voy-je pas une insolente & profane,
Qui gaste de son nid le carquois de Diane?
Une autre a pour abry la harpe d'Apollon:
Cette autre, de Pommone habite un creux melon.
I'admire celle-cy qui simple s'avanture
De confier sa race à ce larron Mercure.
(*Les promenades de Richelieu,* IVe Promenade, 22)

Perhaps the statue now in a private collection and drawn by Canini (see Montembault and Schloder, *L'album Canini,* 176–77, no. 14, figs. 65, 65A).

14. These are the famous *Dying Slave* and *Rebellious Slave* of Michelangelo (Paris, Louvre), both carved in 1513–16 for the Tomb of Julius II. Never put in

place on the tomb, the figures were given by the sculptor in 1544 to Roberto Strozzi (cousin of Catherine de Médicis). Strozzi wanted to give them to the French king, François I, but the latter died in 1547 before this could be done. Strozzi then presented them to his son and successor, Henri II, and the statues arrived in France in 1550. Some time after their arrival, they were given by the French king to the Constable of France, Anne de Montmorency, who installed the statues in niches within a courtyard frontispiece of his château of Écouen. In 1632, on the eve of his execution, Henri II de Montmorency (the Constable's son) willed them to Cardinal Richelieu, and they were displayed at the cardinal's château (see below, n. 15); in the eighteenth century the Maréchal de Richelieu (the cardinal's great-nephew) had them removed to Paris. The sculptures were acquired by the French government in 1794. For the history of these works in eighteenth-century France, see Giorgio Vasari, *La vita di Michelangelo nelle redazioni del 1550 e del 1568*, ed. Paola Barocchi (Milan and Naples: Riccardo Ricciardi, 1962), 2:316–17.

15. Mlle. de Montpensier, who visited the château in 1637, reported: "Il y a au haut du degré un balcon qui donne sur la cour, où sont deux esclaves en figure de bronze [sic] pris à Écouen, qui étoit à M. de Montmorency, que l'on tient les deux plus rares pièces de cette nature qu'on ait vues de notre siècle" (*Mémoires*, ed. Chéruel, 1:24). Marot depicted this balcony, with the *Slaves* above in niches on the *premier étage* of the central pavilion of the *corps-de-logis*, facing the courtyard; they formed a continuous sequence with antique statues placed in niches along the length of that floor to left and right (one statue was labeled "Apollon belissime antique")(*Le magnifique chasteau de Richelieu*, M15; repr. in Goldfarb, ed., *Richelieu: Art and Power*, 252, fig. 4). This was the original arrangement, which echoed the exterior placement of the *Slaves* on a courtyard façade at Écouen. Clearly, the installation at Richelieu was meant to vaunt Michelangelo's works as equal, and perhaps superior, to ancient statuary.

Julien Collardeau, in the earliest description of the château (*La description de Richelieu, à la mémoire du Cardinal-Duc*, n.p., n.d.; published shortly after 1642), penned lines which mostly apply to the *Rebellious Slave*:

> On voit roidir leurs nerfs, on voit grossir leurs veines:
> Voi[s] ce col détourné, ce pied droit suspendu,
> Ce coude replié, ce bras gauche étendu;
> La cruauté de l'art fait plaindre la nature
> De tenir si long-temps leur corps à la torture:
> Les noeuds que vainement ils tâchent d'arracher,
> Les serrent jusqu'aux os, & meurtrissent la chair;
> Leurs yeux sont gros de pleurs, & leur visage exprime
> La grandeur de leur peine, & l'horreur de leur crime.
>
> (As quoted in Claude-Pierre Goujet, *Bibliothèque françoise ou Histoire de la littérature françoise* . . . [Paris: Hippolyte-Louis Guerin & P. G. Le Mercier, 1754], 16:27; I have been unable to locate a copy of Collardeau's poem.)

Desmarets wrote of the *Slaves* in 1653:

> Et ces nobles Captifs vivans dans la sculpture,
> Dont l'un brave le sort, l'autre triste l'endure;
> En qui ses derniers coups l'art voulut reserver,
> Deffiant l'avenir d'oser les achever.
> (*Les promenades de Richelieu*, Ier Promenade, 3)

At some date between Marot's publication (ca. 1650) and La Fontaine's visit (1663), the *Slaves* were moved to the interior of the château, to the ground floor of the main staircage, located in the center of the *corps-de-logis*. Between the two flights of an "imperial stair" was a vestibule with three niches on each side; Michelangelo's *Slaves* were placed facing each other, probably in the central niches (see plan in Aubineau, *Richelieu. "Par ordre du Cardinal . . ."* 33). La Fontaine is unambiguous about their location: "On les a placés en lieu remarquable, c'est-à-dire à l'endroit du grand degré, l'un d'un côté du vestibule, l'autre de l'autre" (Caudal, ed., *Lettres de La Fontaine*, 61). He furthermore noted that he did not ascend the main stair (which led to the balcony, where the *Slaves* had originally been installed).

However, the sculptures were evidently moved back to their balcony by 1676, as reported by Vignier (*Le chasteau de Richelieu*, 1681 ed., 23):

> *Sur le Balcon qui est devant le Dôme du grand Escalier, les deux Esclaves de Michel l'Ange.*
>
> *Premier Esclave.* [Dying Slave]
> C'est dans l'adversité que paroît le courage,
>   Un Homme généreux voit les fers sans frémir,
>   Il est libre dans l'esclavage,
>   Et soufre ses maux sans gémir.
>   *Deuxiéme Esclave.* [Rebellious Slave]
> Vn Esclave dans la fureur,
>   Qui n'écoute rien que sa rage,
> Ne fait qu'augmenter son mal-heur,
>   Et par l'excés de sa douleur,
> Témoigner son peu de courage.

These transfers took place under the Duc de Richelieu.

In 1665, Gianlorenzo Bernini, then in France, mentioned the *Slaves* to his guide, Paul Fréart de Chantelou, who called them "Michelangelo's best works" (*Diary of the Cavaliere Bernini's Visit*, 250). On Michelangelo's reputation in France, see Eugen Dörken, *Geschichte des französischen Michelangelobildes von der Renaissance bis zu Rodin* (Bochum-Langendreer: H. Pöppinghaus, 1936).

16. La Fontaine first wrote: "Pauvres captifs! car cela se peut dire" (Régnier, ed., *Oeuvres de J. de La Fontaine*, 9:264n4). The lover as captive occurs elsewhere in La Fontaine: see Élégie II, v. 3, where are mentioned "nouveaux fers" imposed by Amour; Ballade XII ("Sur le mal d'amour," lines 16, 41–42), and elsewhere (ibid., 9:264n6).

17. Both figures have roughed-out rear supports visible in frontal views. The

form at the rear of the *Dying Slave* was certainly intended as an ape, suggesting the conceit of "ars simia naturae," consistent with Condivi's explanation of the *Slaves* as embodiments of the Liberal Arts; the beginnings of another ape may be present at the rear of the *Rebellious Slave* (for good reproductions of these unfinished passages, see Erwin Panofsky, *Tomb Sculpture* [New York: Harry N. Abrams, 1964], figs. 425, 426). These works would then have represented Painting and Sculpture. Condivi wrote (1553): [The statues bound as captives] "represented the liberal arts, such as painting, sculpture, and architecture, each with its attributes so that it could easily be recognized for what it was, signifying thereby that all the artistic virtues were prisoners of death together with Pope Julius, as they would never find another to favor and foster them as he did" (Ascanio Condivi, *The Life of Michelangelo,* trans. Alice Sedgwick Wohl, ed. Hellmut Wohl [Baton Rouge: Louisiana State University Press, 1976], 33).

On the question of the unfinished in Michelangelo, see Juergen Schulz, "Michelangelo's Unfinished Works," *Art Bulletin* 57 (1975): 366–73 (who holds that the artist, like all others during the Renaissance, always wanted to finish his works); and Howard Hibbard, *Michelangelo,* 2nd ed. (Cambridge: Harper & Row, 1974), 192–93 (who argues that Michelangelo appreciated the expressiveness of the unfinished). Commentary on the question, with extracts from early sources, is provided in Vasari, *La vita di Michelangelo,* ed. Barocchi, 4:1645–70.

18. These lines recall a passage in Pliny the Elder's *Natural History* (35.145), which is worth quoting here; it is uncertain whether La Fontaine had read the ancient author: "Indeed it is an extremely unusual fact and worth remembering that the last works of artists and their unfinished pictures, such as the *Iris* of Aristeides, the *Tyndaridai* of Nikomachos, the *Medea* of Timomachos, and the *Aphrodite* of Apelles . . . are held in greater admiration than finished works; for in these the sketch-lines remain and the actual thoughts of the artists are visible; consequently even in the allurement of commendation, there is sadness because the artist's hand was stilled, while he was working on the picture" (J. J. Pollitt, *The Art of Greece, 1400–31 B.C. Sources and Documents* [Englewood Cliffs, NJ: Prentice-Hall, 1965], 229). I thank Professor Creighton Gilbert for this reference.

19. Desmarets de Saint-Sorlin wrote of the main stair:

> Quand du riche escalier que l'Estranger admire,
> Aux deux larges rempans de marbre & de porphyre,
> J'entre en la vaste court, [etc.]
> (*Les promenades de Richelieu,* IVe Promenade, 22)

20. On the paintings in the château, see John E. Schloder, "La peinture au château de Richelieu," diss., Université de Paris-Sorbonne, 1988; Schnapper, *Curieux du grand siècle,* 141–43.

21. According to Vignier (*Le chasteau de Richelieu*), portraits of Richelieu's grandfather, father, and mother were in the Antichambre (93); a portrait of the cardinal was over the fireplace of the Chambre (94–95).

22. Armand-Jean Vignerot, duc de Richelieu et de Fronsac (1629–1715).

23. Armand de Maillé-Brézé, duc de Fronsac et de Caumont was the cardinal's nephew. He succeeded to Richelieu's maritime offices (see above, Letter V, n8)

in 1643 and was killed during a naval engagement in 1646 at the age of twenty-seven. He was the brother-in-law of the Grand Condé.

24. La Fontaine at first wrote but then crossed out: "Je consideray aussi avec grande attention le feu marquis de Richelieu." Jean-Baptiste-Amador Vignerot, marquis de Richelieu (1632–62) was the brother of Armand-Jean Vignerot and lieutenant-general of the king's armies. In 1652 he married Jeanne-Baptiste de Beauvais, a daughter of Madame de Beauvais, first lady-in-waiting to Anne of Austria.

25. Emmanuel-Joseph Vignerot, comte de Richelieu, abbé de Marmoutier et de Saint-Ouen de Rouen (1639–65), brother of Armand-Jean and Jean-Baptiste-Amador Vignerot. Although an abbé, he fought as a soldier for Louis XIV against the Turks in 1664, then offered his military services to the Republic of Venice but died there in 1665.

26. La Fontaine at first wrote but then crossed out: "Par une fatalité dont tous ceux qui connoissent son mérite n'iront point chercher la cause dans les astres" (Régnier, ed., *Oeuvres de J. de La Fontaine*, 9:268n2).

27. La Fontaine is alluding to royal mistresses: "Belle-Agnès" is Agnès Sorel (1422–50), mistress of Charles VII. "Joconde" is a reference to Leonardo da Vinci's *Mona Lisa* that had been in the collection of François I at Fontainebleau (probably still there in 1663); it was thought by some that the sitter was that king's mistress. Pierre Dan wrote that *Mona Lisa* was "le portrait d'vne vertueuse Dame Italienne, & non pas d'vne Courtisane (comme quelques-vns croyent) nommée *Mona Lissa*, vulgairement appellée Ioconde" (*Le trésor des merveilles de la maison royale de Fontainebleau* . . . [Paris: S. Cramoisy, 1642], 135–36). Mona Lisa's real name was Lisa Gherardini del Giocondo, the wife of Francesco del Giocondo.

La Fontaine's viewing of portraits of royal mistresses and his comment about their power later found expression in the description of Cupid's palace in his *Les Amours de Psyché et de Cupidon* (1669):

> Pour servir d'ornement à ses divers étages,
> L'architecte y posa les vivantes images
> De ces objets divins, Cléopâtres, Phrynés,
> Par qui sont les héros en triomphe menés.
> (Ed. used: [Paris: Plon, 1960], 43)

28. The Grand Cabinet or Cabinet du Roi occupied a corner pavilion of the right-hand part of the *corps-de-logis*, which housed the king's apartment. On the paintings which decorated the Cabinet, see Schnapper, *Curieux du grand siècle*, 142–43. The most distinguished were those from the Studiolo of Isabella d'Este in the Castello di San Giorgio at Mantua (works by Mantegna, Perugino, and Costa), and three by Poussin (see below, n29). On the Mantuan pictures, see Egon Verheyen, *The Paintings in the "Studiolo" of Isabella d'Este at Mantua* (New York: New York University Press, 1971). Richelieu probably acquired these by 1630.

Desmarets de Saint-Sorlin also described the Grand Cabinet (VIIIe Promenade, 57–58) and wrote of the paintings:

> Plus haut voyez de l'art les plus rares effets.
> Ces tableaux merveilleux, ces chef-d'oeuvres parfaits.

> Icy du grand Poussin la mignardise regne,
> Du Perusin charmant, & du docte Mantegne,
> Et d'autres dont le trait par l'oeuvre est ennobly;
> (*Les promenades de Richelieu,* VIIIe Promenade, 58)

29. These were the *Triumph of Bacchus* (Kansas City, Nelson-Atkins Museum of Art), the *Triumph of Pan* (London, National Gallery), and the *Triumph of Silenus* (National Gallery, London; perhaps a copy). The first two pictures were commissioned by Richelieu in 1634/35 and sent to him from Rome in 1636; the *Silenus* followed soon afterward. See Hugh Macandrew and Hugh Brigstocke, *Poussin, Sacraments and Bacchanals,* exhib. cat. (Edinburgh: National Gallery of Scotland, 1981); Goldfarb, ed., *Richelieu: Art and Power,* 292–98, nos. 126–28.

Desmarets de Saint-Sorlin described the *Triumph of Bacchus* (*Les promenades de Richelieu,* VIIIe Promenade, 58):

> Voyez le riche amas des diverses postures,
> Le char orné de pampre où triomphe Baccus
> Des peuples du Matin par son tyrse vaincus.
> Voyez la fureur gaye, & les folles boutades
> Des Satyres cornus, & des belles Menades.

30. On this work, see Verheyen, *The Paintings in the "Studiolo" of Isabella d'Este,* 41–44, pl. 24.

31. La Fontaine's description of this painting is very confused, an indication that he was writing from a flawed memory. In the center of the painting, Venus (Love), bareheaded and holding a long flaming torch (and identified by a sign labelled "VENERI" at her feet), fights with Diana (Chastity), armed with bow and arrow. La Fontaine had apparently remembered the figure of Minerva at the left, wearing armor and a helmet and brandishing a javelin against a Cupid. The description by Desmarets de Saint-Sorlin is even more confused:

> L'ouvrage en l'autre quadre est beau, mais serieux,
> Où la sage Pallas, d'un regard furieux,
> Seule combat Venus, les Amours & les Graces,
> Qui tombent sous son fer desja foibles et lasses.
> Que ce peintre est trompeur! la Grace a l'oeil mignard
> En son tableau succombe, & triomphe en son art.
> (*Les promenades de Richelieu,* VIIIe Promenade, 58)

32. A strange comment: Minerva, whom La Fontaine apparently confused with Venus, is not wounded, but is about to slay a Cupid; the real Venus is not wounded either. However, it is curious to note that Isabella d'Este, in her instructions to Perugino drawn up on 19 January 1503, specified that "Venus has been struck by Diana's arrow only on the surface of the body, on her crown and garland, or on a veil she may have around her; and part of Diana's raiment will have been singed by the torch of Venus, but nowhere else will either of them have been wounded" (D. S. Chambers, ed., *Patrons and Artists in the Italian Renaissance* [Columbia: University of South Carolina Press, 1971], 136). Perugino chose to omit Venus's crown and garland, painted a veiled garment about her, but avoided any apparent

wounds about the goddess (although she is about to be struck by Diana's arrow). For a good color reproduction of Venus, see Vittoria Garibaldi, *Perugino: Catalogo completo* (Florence: Octavo, 1999), 72.

33. The *Four Elements* (Earth, Air, Fire, Water)(Orléans, Musée des Beaux-Arts), painted by Claude Deruet about 1640–42. On this series, see Mary O'Neill, *Musée des beaux-arts d'Orléans. Les peintures de l'école française des XVIIe et XVIIIe siècles* (Orléans: Musée des beaux-arts, 1981), 1:47–49; Goldfarb, ed., *Richelieu: Art and Power*, 315–17, nos. 138, 139. The series decorated the Cabinet de la Reine.

34. Fireworks (*Fire*); "Tilting at the Ring" (Homage to Anne of Austria and her two sons)(*Earth*); "Carrousels" (Falcon-Hunting) (*Air*); Amusements with Sleds (*Water*). The four pictures are illustrated in O'Neill (as in n33), 2:pls. 28–31; *Water* and *Fire* in Goldfarb, ed. (as in n33), 317 (in color).

35. On this painting, whose author is never mentioned in the sources, see Schloder, "La peinture au château de Richelieu," 144, 590–92. It was not the *Saint Francis* by Sebastiano del Piombo after a design by Michelangelo, bequeathed by Montmorency to Cardinal Richelieu along with the *Slaves* for the Julius tomb (see above, n14), and placed in the cardinal's Chambre. See ibid., 556–57.

36. On this work, undoubtedly a copy after Titian, see ibid., 559–60. It was in a small chapel of the Antichambre of the cardinal, "toute remplie de Tableaux, dont la plus grande partie sont de bonnes copies d'aprés Raphaël d'Vrbain, & le Titian" (Vignier, *Le chasteau de Richelieu*, 94).

37. Marot (*Le magnifique chasteau de Richelieu*, M16) noted the chapel: "Oratoire ou il y a un St Hierosme à la Mozaique ouvrage tres-rare." The mosaic was briefly described by Claude Perrault (*Voyage à Bordeaux,* 151–52): "Dans la chapelle, il y a un tableau d'un *Saint-Jérôme* qui est fait en mosaïque. Les pierres, dont elle est composée, ne sont pas larges d'une ligne et épaisses de demi-ligne, ainsi que l'on pouvoit voir en un endroit qui étoit éraillé." Vignier also commented on it (*Le chasteau de Richelieu*, 94): "Mais on ne peut assez estimer un Saint HIEROSME dans un Paysage, qui est de pierres rapportées, le tout si artistement, qu'il y a peu de personnes qui ne le croyent peint, encore qu'il n'y ait pas un coup de pinceau dans tout le Tableau." This micro-mosaic has not been identified.

38. La Fontaine used the verb *niveller* (*mettre de niveau*), which can mean "to create a mosaic." It also can mean "to amuse oneself with trifles" (*s'amuser à des vétilles, à des niaiseries, à des bagatelles*).

39. La Fontaine wrote "nivèlerie," playing upon the secondary meaning indicated in n38.

40. La Fontaine wrote "un nivelier," again playing upon the word.

41. This table is now in the Galerie d'Apollon in the Louvre. Marot (*Le magnifique chasteau de Richelieu*, M18) wrote: "Dans le Milieu dudit Salon, il y a une Table de pierres pretieuses de raport, entre-autre, une Agathe d'une prodigieuse grandeur la fait estimer une des plus belles tables du monde." It was described by Desmarets de Saint-Sorlin:

> Cette table est de jaspe; et tous ses ornemens
> Ces delicates fleurs, & ces compartimens,
> Sont formez d'un amas de pierres precieuses

> Que tailla le bel art des mains laborieuses,
> Qui de la pierre mesme efleurent les couleurs,
> Dont se fit sans pinceau la nuance des fleurs.
> L'Art imite souvent les corps de la Nature:
> Icy d'un corps solide il forme une peinture.
> (*Les promenades de Richelieu*, VIIIe Promenade, 60)

The table is perhaps Roman, of the last quarter of the sixteenth century. It measures almost two meters in length, 1.30 m. wide; illus. of the tabletop in Claire Lesage, ed., *Jean de La Fontaine*, exhib. cat., (Paris: Bibliothèque Nationale de France/Seuil, 1995), 55, center.

42. A very detailed description of the semiprecious stones adorning this table is given by Vignier (*Le chasteau de Richelieu*, 100–101), who notes that it stood at the entrance to the Galerie.

43. The famous agate of Pyrrhus, king of Epirus, engraved with the Nine Muses and Apollo with his lyre.

44. Gautier de Costes, seigneur de la Calprenède de Tolgou et de Vatimesnil, author of the novels *Cléopâtre* (1642) and *Cassandre* (1645). He died in October 1663, only a few weeks after La Fontaine wrote his letter.

45. "La valeur d'Alexandre en ce buste respire" (Desmarets de Saint-Sorlin, *Les promenades de Richelieu*, VIIIe Promenade, 62).

46. Perhaps the anonymous painting now in the Musée de Richelieu (Aubineau, Richelieu. "*Par ordre du Cardinal . . . ,*" illus. on 14).

47. The Galerie des Batailles is described by Vignier (*Le chasteau de Richelieu*, pp. 97ff.). Twelve of the original twenty paintings are now in the Musée National du Château de Versailles; they depict the great battles waged during the ministry of Richelieu. See Schloder, "La peinture au château de Richelieu," 380ff. and 538; Schloder questions their traditional attribution to Michel Dorigny.

48. La Fontaine is describing the crescent-shaped hedge between the (extant) grottoes, which was cut into niches housing statues (see Marot, *Le magnifique chasteau de Richelieu*, M8). Almost all the statues mentioned by La Fontaine are listed as at that garden location by Marot and by Vignier (*Le chasteau de Richelieu*, 149–56).

49. Comme au soir, lorsque l'ombre arrive en un séjour.
     Ou lorsqu'il n'est plus nuit et n'est pas encor jour.

La Fontaine reused the second line of verse in the "Discours à M. le Duc de la Rochefoucauld" ("Les Lapins") (*Fables*, bk. 10, fable 14, line 13.):

> Et que, n'étant plus nuit, il n'est pas encor jour.
> The line is taken from Ovid:
> Aut ubi nox abiit nec tamen orta dies.
> (*Amores*, 1.5.6)

50. A reference to the conquest of Artois in 1640 and the ceding of Roussillon to France by the Treaty of the Pyrenees in 1659.

51. A reference to the dike of La Rochelle, built 1626–27.

52. The English.

53. Again, the English?
54. The poets.
55. La Fontaine and M. de Châteauneuf had promised M. Jannart to meet him the next day at Châtellerault (see Letter IV).
56. Châteauneuf's breeches and high boots (see below) marked him as a royal police officer.

Letter VI

1. Because the visit to the château of Richelieu lasted into the evening, La Fontaine and M. de Châteauneuf had to sleep in the town, then arise very early to meet Jannart at Châtellerault (see above, Letter V, n55).
2. Poussart de Vigean, marquis de Faure (or Fors), brother of the Duchesse de Richelieu, murdered in 1663 near his sister's château near Poitiers. See Charles Athanase Walckenaër, *Histoire de la vie et des ouvrages de J. de La Fontaine*, 4th ed. (Paris: Firmin Didot, 1858), 1:123–31.
3. The Pidoux were La Fontaine's mother's family.
4. La Fontaine himself had a long nose.
5. The longevity of the Pidoux was an established fact; see Régnier, ed., *Oeuvres de J. de La Fontaine*, 9:284–85n4.
6. René Pidoux du Verger (b. 1581).
7. "La Fontaine, pourtant lecteur de romans, estime, avec la plupart des moralistes de son temps, que ces ouvrages portent à l'amour passionné et sont plus funestes qu'utiles aux femmes et jeunes filles" (Caudal, ed., *Lettres de La Fontaine*,156n38). Cf. François de Salignac de la Mothe-Fénelon, *De l'éducation des filles* [1687], chap. 2 (in his *Oeuvres*, ed. Jacques Le Brun [Paris: Gallimard, 1983], 1:95; see also 1:1272 [n2 for 95] for an informative note by Le Brun on negative attitudes toward novels in seventeenth-century France).
8. A large town, underpopulated and badly built or fortified.
9. The Pierre-Levée and the Passe-Lourdin are actual rocks near Poitiers, the former set up in 1478 to mark the annual fair, the latter ancient, and used by the university students in a ritual. Interesting information about these rocks is given in Régnier, 9:287–88 nn8 and 1. Rabelais was aware of the connection of the Passe-Lourdin and the students of the university of Poitiers, and incorporated this in *Gargantua et Pantagruel*, bk. 2, chap. 5.
10. Perhaps La Barigny or another beauty.
11. "Car au départ il se faut pendre": The expression "après cela il faut se pendre" se dit quand on a manqué une belle occasion" (É. Littré, *Dictionnaire de la langue française* [Paris: Hachette, 1882], 3: 1041, r. col.).
12. An allusion to the theme of the Mountain of Virtue, first adumbrated in Hesiod, *Works and Days*, lines 286–92. See Erwin Panofsky, *Hercule à la croisée des chemins et autres matériaux figuratifs de l'Antiquité dans l'art plus récent*, trans. Danièle Cohn (Paris: Flammarion, 1999), 59, 60. [1st German ed. 1930]. Interestingly, the motif appears in Deruet's *Water* from the *Four Elements* series, which La Fontaine had just seen in the Château de Richelieu (see above, Letter V, nn33, 34; illus. in Goldfarb, ed., *Richelieu: Art and Power*, 317, no. 138, and

NOTES

detail facing Acknowledgements page). In this painting, Cardinal Richelieu stands at the entrance to a Temple of Fame, set atop the mountain; the themes of Virtue and Fame are frequently interchanged in this iconography.

A Christian reworking of this theme (the Mountain of Faith which leads to God) is found in Desmarets de Saint-Sorlin, *Les promenades de Richelieu,* Ier Promenade, 4–5.

13. This incident actually happened in 1634.

14. La Fontaine wrote "second étage," but in the sixteenth and seventeenth centuries, the *premier étage* was sometimes referred to as the *second étage,* and this is undoubtedly where the kitchen was located.

15. The king thought he had been poisoned.

16. La Fontaine was now in the region where the *patois poitevin,* a dialect of the *langue d'oïl,* was spoken.

In a humorous letter to La Fontaine written at Uzès (11 November 1661; see Introduction), Jean Racine noted that after leaving Lyon and traveling south along the Rhône to Vienne and Valence on his way to Uzès, he found it progressively more difficult to understand the local language and to make himself understood in French. Racine was hearing Occitan, which he perceived to be a mixture of Spanish and Italian (Jean Racine, *Lettres d'Uzès,* ed. Jean Dubu [Uzès: Ateliers Henri Peladan, 1963], 3; see also 5n4 for Dubu's analysis of how Racine's use of the French word *broquette* [carpet tack] was misinterpreted as *brouketô,* the Occitan word for matches). The reports of these writers testify to the fact that France was far from being linguistically unified by the 1660s.

La Fontaine's wife was related to Racine's family, and she probably played a role in bringing the two young writers in contact about 1660 (Wadsworth, *Young La Fontaine,* 17).

17. The faithful companion of Aeneas.

18. A letter that apparently was never written.

19. François de La Fayette, abbé de Sainte-Marie de Dalon, bishop of Limoges, first chaplain to Anne of Austria (d. 1678). The husband of Madame de La Fayette (author of *La Princesse de Clèves*) was this bishop's nephew.

20. "Il est curieux de rapprocher cette opinion de La Fontaine d'un propos très ancien, que l'on prête au roi Charles VII; celui-ci passant à Limoges fut choqué, dit-on, de la simplicité des vêtements des femmes qui ne suivaient pas la mode, de leurs coiffures qui les rendaient disgracieuses, et leur en fit le repoche" (Camille Jouhanneaud, "Le voyage de La Fontaine en Limousin," *Bulletin de la Société archéologique et historique du Limousin* 63 [1913]: 227n1).

21. Probably meaning a good wine from Saint-Mesmin in Champagne, La Fontaine's home region.

22. In disparaging Limoges, La Fontaine continued a tradition among French writers going back to Rabelais (see Caudal, ed., *Lettres de La Fontaine,* 162n81).

Bibliography

HISTORY AND EDITIONS OF THE LETTERS

La Fontaine's letters to his wife remained in his family and were unpublished during his lifetime. Letters I–IV first appeared in *Oeuvres diverses de M. de La Fontaine de l'Académie françoise* (Paris: Didot, 1729), 2:26–56; this was twenty years after the death of Madame de La Fontaine. Caudal's edition (see below) reproduces these, with modernized accentuation and punctuation. The original mss. for Letters I–IV are lost, but the autographs of Letters V and VI are preserved in Paris, Bibliothèque de l'Arsenal, mss. Conrart, no. 5132 [Letter V], pp. 123–39 and no. 5131 [Letter VI], pp. 875–81; these are published by Caudal. A manuscript page from Letter V is reproduced in *Lettres à sa femme. Voyage de Paris en Limousin*, preface by Michel Mourlet (Paris: Valmonde-Tredaniel, 1995), facing XVI.

Letters V and VI were first printed in Louis-Jean-Nicolas Monmerqué, ed., *Opuscules inédits de La Fontaine* (Paris, J.-J. Blaise, 1820), 15–48, and in Philippe-Emmanuel de Coulanges, *Mémoires . . .* (Paris: J.-J. Blaise, 1820), 568–608. In that same year, all six letters were published together for the first time by Charles Athanase Walckenaër, *Nouvelles oeuvres diverses de Jean de La Fontaine . . .* (Paris: A. Nepveu, 1820).

I have used the following edition: Ange-Marie Caudal, ed., *Lettres de La Fontaine à sa femme ou Relation d'un voyage de Paris en Limousin* (Paris: Centre de documentation universitaire, 1966) (hereafter referred to as Caudal). This is a scholarly (although poorly produced) publication, provided with abundant and very helpful notes. My paragraph divisions follow this edition, with modernized punctuation and place-names. Also essential is the older standard edition by Henri Régnier, *Oeuvres de J. de La Fontaine,* new ed. (Paris: Librairie Hachette, 1892), 9:219–95. Of great value are the notes to the Letters in the edition by Pierre Clarac: Jean de La Fontaine, *Oeuvres diverses* (Paris: Bibliothèque de la Pléiade, 1942), 898–911. Other later editions of the letters to 1966 are listed by Caudal, 188–94.

ON TRAVEL AND TRAVEL WRITING IN FRANCE

Doiron, Normand. *L'art de voyager. Le déplacement à l'époque classique.* Sainte-Foy and Paris: Les Presses de l'Université Laval and Klincksieck, 1995.

Wolfzettel, Friedrich. *Le discours du voyageur. Pour une histoire littéraire du récit de voyage en France du moyen âge au XVIIIe siècle.* Paris: Presses universitaires de France, 1996. (Discussion of La Fontaine's *Voyage* on 227–30)

SELECTED WRITINGS ON THE LETTERS AND RELATED MATTERS (BY DATE)

(See the bibliographies in Caudal, 194–97, especially for the older literature.)

Petit, Léon. "Autour du procès Fouquet. La Fontaine et son oncle Jannart sous la griffe de Colbert." *Revue d'histoire littéraire de la France* 47 (1947): 193–210.

Wadsworth, Philip A. *Young La Fontaine: A Study of his Artistic Growth in his Early Poetry and First Fables.* Evanston, IL: Northwestern University Press, 1952, 118–28.

Caudal (1966), esp. chaps. I and IV.

Collinet, Jean-Pierre. *Le monde littéraire de La Fontaine.* Paris: P.U.F., 1970, chap. 3 ("Le Voyage").

Shaw, David. "La Fontaine's Letters to His Wife." *Modern Languages* 53 (1972): 125–32.

Defrenne, Madeleine. "Le phénomène créateur chez La Fontaine: le poète et le monde." *Australian Journal of French Studies* 12 (1975): 119–67.

Orieux, Jean. *La Fontaine ou la vie est un conte.* Paris: Flammarion, 1976, 206ff.

Chupeau, Jacques. "Les récits de voyages. Aux lisières du roman." *Revue d'histoire littéraire de la France* 77, nos. 3–4 (May/August 1977): 536–53.

Zobeidah, Youssef. "La Fontaine et la poésie de l'eau: Relation d'un voyage de Paris en Limousin." *Les Lettres Romanes* 33, no. 2 (1979), 173–95.

Collinet, Jean-Pierre. "Le voyage de La Fontaine dans le Limousin. La découverte de la France." In *La découverte de la France au XVIIe siècle. Colloques internationaux du C.N.R.S.* Paris: C.N.R.S., 1980, 43–49.

Defrenne, Madeleine. "La Fontaine à la découverte du Limousin et d'un mode d'écriture." In ibid., 51–58.

Duchêne, Roger. *La Fontaine.* Paris: Fayard, 1990, chap. 26 ("Le voyage en Limousin").

———. "Un exemple de lettres galantes: La *Relation d'un voyage de Paris en Limousin* de La Fontaine." *Papers on French Seventeenth Century Literature* 23 (1996): 57–71.

Morgante, Jole. "À la croisée des genres: Les 'Lettres à sa femme' de La Fontaine." In *Vie des salons et activités littéraires de Marguerite de Valois à Mme de Staël: Actes du colloque international de Nancy (6–8 octobre 1999),* ed. Roger Marchal, 271–83. Nancy: Presses universitaires de Nancy, 2001.

Index

Aesop, 11
Alemán, Mateo, 18, 75 n. 7
Alexander the Great, 47, 58, 85 n. 45
Amboise, château, 14, 17, 43–44, 74 nn. 1 and 3; town, 43, 44
Aubigné, Agrippa d', 18, 73 n. 5

Beauce, 14, 33, 37, 39, 73 n. 7
Bellac, 16, 24, 65–67
Blésois, 39
Blois, château, 38, 40, 73 n. 10; town, 14, 38–39; Saint-Louis, 73 n. 6, Saint-Solenne, 38, 73 n. 6
Boccaccio, Giovanni, 11
Bourg-la-Reine, 15, 30, 31

Calprenède, Gautier de Costes de la, 58, 85 n. 44
Candé, Brodeau de, 32, 70 n. 5
Chapelain, Jean, 18, 35, 71 n. 17, 75 n. 7
Charles VII (king of France), 20, 35, 71 n. 15, 72 n. 2, 73 n. 4, 82 n. 27, 87 n. 20
Charles the Bold (duke of Burgundy), 37, 72 n. 3
Charonne, 29
Châteauneuf, Monsieur de (royal officer), 15, 16, 30, 34, 35, 38, 40, 46, 49, 53, 59, 60, 61, 62, 65, 67, 86 nn. 55 and 56, 86 n. 1 (Letter VI)
Château-Thierry, 12, 14, 22
Châtellerault, 15, 16, 23, 46, 62–64, 65, 86 nn. 55 and 56, 86 n. 1 (Letter VI)
Châtres (Arpajon), 32, 70 n. 6
Chauvigny, 16, 65, 66
Cher, River, 44, 45
Chilly-Mazarin, 31
Clamart, 29, 31

Cléry, Notre-Dame, 14, 37, 72 n. 2; tomb of Louis XI, 14, 37, 72 n. 2
Cocatrix, Valley, 32
Colbert, Jean-Baptiste, 13, 14
Collardeau, Julien, 17, 79 n. 15
Coulanges, Philippe-Emmanuel de, 24
Creuse River, 44

Deruet, Claude, 21, 84 n. 33, 86 n. 12
Desmarets de Saint-Sorlin, Jean, 17–19, 49, 52, 53, 76–77 n. 2, 77 n. 6, 78 n. 13, 80 n. 15, 81 n. 19, 82 n. 28, 83 nn. 29 and 31, 84–85 n. 41, 85 n. 45, 87 n. 12
Dürer, Albrecht, 53

Étampes, 33, 70 n. 12

Faure, Poussart de Vigean, marquis de, 62, 86 n. 2
Félibien, André, 13, 18, 76 n. 1
Ferté-Milon, 22
Florence, Palazzo Pitti, 58
Fontainebleau, château, 20, 82 n. 27
Foucquet, Nicolas, 12, 15, 17, 44, 73 n. 13, 74 n. 6, 78 n. 11
François I (king of France), 20, 40, 74 n. 5, 79 n. 14, 82 n. 27
Fronde, 33, 70 n. 12, 77 n. 6

Gaston d'Orléans, 38, 40, 73 n. 11

Henri IV (king of France), 20, 54
Héricart, Marie (wife of La Fontaine), 12–15, 22–24, 87 n. 16
Héricart, Marie (aunt of La Fontaine's wife), 31, 69 n. 1
Hermite, Louis-Tristan l', 37, 73 n. 4

Indre River, 44, 45

INDEX

Jannart, Jacques, 12–16, 22, 28, 29, 31, 32, 34, 38, 54, 62, 66, 67, 86 n. 55, 86 n. 1 (Letter VI)
Joan of Arc, 14; monument, Orléans, 14, 35, 71 n. 15

La Fayette, François de, 67, 87 n. 19
La Fayette, Madame de, 23
La Fontaine, Charles de (father of Jean), 12
La Fontaine, Charles de (son of Jean), 30, 69 n. 7
La Fontaine, Jean de, works of: *Adonis*, 12; *Amours de Psyché et de Cupidon, les*, 11, 82 n. 27; *Ballade XII*, 80 n. 16; *Contes et nouvelles en vers*, 11, 22; *Élégie II*, 80 n. 15; *Élégie aux nymphes de Vaux*, 74 n. 6; *Eunuque, l'*, 12; *Fables*, 11, 17, 22, 70 nn. 9 and 11, 73 n. 9, 74 n. 4, 75, n. 10, 85 n. 49; *Nouveaux contes*, 11; *Ode au Roi*, 74 n. 6; *Songe de Vaux, le*, 12–13, 18, 75 n. 6, 76 n. 1
La Tueterie (La Fontaine's farm), 32, 70 n. 8
Le Brun, Charles, 12
Lemercier, Jacques, 50, 51
Le Nôtre, André, 12
Leonardo da Vinci, 20, 82 n. 27
Le Vau, Louis, 12
Limoges, 12–14, 21–22, 25, 28, 30, 62, 67, 87 nm. 20 and 22
Limousin, 23, 39, 41, 44, 46, 65, 67
Livy, 18, 37
Loire River, 14, 17, 35, 38, 40–42, 44, 47
Loire Valley, 14, 15
Louis XI (king of France), 14, 37, 72 nn. 2 and 3, 73 n. 4
Louis XIII (king of France), 19, 54, 66, 72 n. 2, 77 nn. 4 and 8
Louis XIV (king of France), 13, 14, 33, 82 n. 25
Louis II de Bourbon, prince de Condé (le Grand Condé), 54, 82 n. 23
Luther, Martin, 15, 34
Lyon, 26, 27

Maillé-Brézé, Armand de, 54, 81–82 n. 23

Mansart, François, 14, 73 n. 10
Mantegna, Andrea, 53, 82–83 n. 28
Manthelan (Montels?), 45–46
Marot, Clément, 18, 75 n. 9
Maucroix, François de, 13, 25, 26, 40, 51, 73–74 n. 13, 78 n. 11
Mazarin, Jules Cardinal, 14, 57
Meudon, 29
Michelangelo, 17–19, 52, 78–81 nn. 14–17, 84 n. 35
Molière, 23, 69 n. 3
Mona Lisa (Lisa Gherardini del Giocondo), 20, 54, 82 n. 27
Montlhéry, fortress, 31–32, 70 nn. 3 and 4
Montreuil-sous-Bois, 13
Moulin, Pierre du, 34, 71 n. 13

Orléans, 14, 17, 35–36, 38, 39; Pont Georges V, 71 n. 15, Pont des Tourelles (*see* Joan of Arc, monument); Sainte-Croix, 36
Ovid, 18, 40

Paris, 12–14, 22, 26, 28, 36; Bastille, 13; Hôtel Mazarin, 58; Palais, 69 n. 6, Palais-Cardinal (Palais-Royal), 77 n. 8; Parlement, 12, 14, 69 n. 6; Place Royale (des Vosges), 48; Saint-Eustache, 75 n. 12
Perugino, Pietro, 20, 53, 55, 82–83 n. 28, 83 n. 31, 83–84 n. 32
Pidoux du Verger, René, 16, 63, 86 n. 6
Plessis-Paté, 32, 70 n. 6
Poitiers, 15, 16, 34, 62, 64, 86 n. 9
Port-de-Piles, 31, 46
Poussin, Nicolas, 51, 53, 55, 78 n. 11, 82–83 n. 28, 83 n. 29
Provence, 26

Rabelais, François, 17, 73 n. 7, 86 n. 9, 87 n. 22
Racine, Jean, 25–27, 87 n. 16
Reims, 22
Rhône River, 26, 27
Richelieu, Armand-Jean du Plessis, cardinal de, 15, 17, 19, 46–47, 50, 51, 54, 55, 58–60, 75 n. 12, 77 n. 8, 78 n. 11, 79 n. 14, 87 n. 12

Richelieu, Armand-Jean Vignerot, duc de, 54, 76n. 2, 80n. 15, 81n.22, 82nn. 24 and 25
Richelieu, Emmanuel-Joseph Vignerot, comte de, 54, 82n. 25
Richelieu, Jean-Baptiste-Amador Vignerot, marquis de, 54, 82nn. 24 and 25
Richelieu, town, 15, 17, 46–48, 62; château, 15, 17, 20–21, 23, 25, 42, 47, 49–61 (Letter V), 86nn. 1 and 12
Rome, 13, 45

Saint-Cloud, 29
Saint-Denis, 58, 72n. 2
Saint-Dyé-sur-Loire, 38
Saint-Mandé, House of Nicolas Fouquet, 12
Saintes, 13
Sceaux, 31
Scudéry, Madeleine de, 13, 76n. 1
Seine River, 36, 60
Sévigné, Madame de, 23, 24
Sologne, 36, 37
Sorel, Agnès, 20, 54, 82n. 27

Tallemant des Réaux, 22
Tavannes, Jacques de Saulx, comte de, 33, 70–71n. 12
Terence, 12
Titian, 21, 53, 55, 84n. 36
Torfou, Valley, 32, 70n. 7
Touraine, 15, 39
Tours, 44
Turenne, Henri de la Tour d'Auvergne, vicomte de, 33, 70n. 12

Uzès, 25, 26, 87n. 16

Valence, 27
Vaux-le-Vicomte, château, 12, 13, 22, 26, 49, 74n. 6
Vendômois, 37
Venice, San Marco, 58
Versailles, 11, 12, 18
Vienne, 27
Vienne River, 44, 62–63
Vignier, Benjamin, 17, 80n. 15, 81n. 21, 84n. 37, 85nn. 42 and 47
Virgil, 18, 43, 74n. 4
Voiture, Vincent, 18, 48, 69n. 2, 76n. 16